Transcreation
of the
Bhagavad Gita

Ashok Kumar Malhotra

State University of New York
College at Oneonta

Prentice Hall, Upper Saddle River, NJ 07458

Library of Congress Cataloging-in-Publication Data

Bhagavadgītā. English.
    Transcreation of the Bhagavad Gita / Ashok Kumar Malhotra.
        p.   cm. — (Library of liberal arts)
    ISBN 0–02–374921–0
    I. Malhotra, Ashok Kumar.   II. Title.   III. Series.
BL1138.62.E5   1998
294.5'92404521—dc21   98–9468
                                                            CIP

Editor-in-Chief: Charlyce Jones Owen
Acquisitions Editor: Karita France
Production Editor: Joseph Scordato
Copy Editor: Stephen Hopkins
Manufacturing Buyer: Robert Anderson
Cover Art Director: Jayne Conte

This book was set in 10/12 Baskerville by Stratford Publishing Services, Inc.,
and was printed and bound by Courier Companies. The cover was printed by
Phoenix Color Corp.

© 1999 by Prentice-Hall, Inc.
Simon & Schuster / A Viacom Company
Upper Saddle River, New Jersey 07458

Printed in the United States of America

10 9 8 7 6 5 4 3 2 1

0-02-374921-0

Prentice-Hall International (UK) Limited, *London*
Prentice-Hall of Australia Pty, Limited, *Sydney*
Prentice-Hall Canada Inc., *Toronto*
Prentice-Hall Hispanoamericana, S.A., *Mexico*
Prentice-Hall of India Private Limited, *New Delhi*
Prentice-Hall of Japan, Inc., *Tokyo*
Simon & Schuster Asia Pte. Ltd., *Singapore*
Editora Prentice-Hall do Brasil, Ltda., *Rio de Janeiro*

This translation is dedicated
to the memory
of my Grandfather,
Hari Chand Chopra,
and to my Mother,
Vidya Wati Malhotra,
who is still an inspiring story teller.

Contents

Preface

My involvement with the *Bhagavad Gita* has been at both personal and professional levels. While growing up in India, I was initially introduced to the *Bhagavad Gita* at age five by my maternal grandfather, who was a great story teller and a link to the oral tradition of India. Every evening when my grandfather returned from work, he sat down in a cane chair and while puffing on his hubble-bubble pipe, he told me and the other grandchildren stories from the *Ramayana, Mahabharata,* and *Panchatantra,* and he would also recite the Buddhist *Jataka Tales.*

My interest in the *Bhagavad Gita* was further enhanced by my mother, who read a chapter of the *Bhagavad Gita* each day, inspiring me to do the same. By the time I had finished high school, I had read the *Bhagavad Gita* for at least ten years on a regular basis and had almost memorized the entire text. My grandfather had repeatedly told us that whenever we were distressed or confused we should read different chapters of the *Bhagavad Gita,* and that this would surely help us resolve the uncertainty and confusion. My mother reiterated the same in a slightly different way. According to her, whenever we were indecisive about two competing and opposite courses of action involving the same situation, we needed to read the section on Arjuna's dilemma and how he resolved it. My grandfather and mother assured us that since both of them found great comfort from the *Bhagavad Gita* in times of turmoil and indecision, we could also reap similar benefits from reading it. These lessons were very instructive.

As a college student, I read more than two dozen English translations of the *Bhagavad Gita* by both Indian and Western scholars. During the past 30 years of teaching the *Bhagavad Gita* to undergraduate students in the United States, I tried various translations. None of them, however, were completely satisfactory for the students or for me. Some of the translations were too literal, while others used old English and were downright incomprehensible— teaching the *Bhagavad Gita* to the undergraduate students became a frustrating task. Though students were interested in learning about this great Hindu text, they were turned off because of the misconstrued translations which never addressed the needs of the students at a grass-roots level. I recalled when my grandfather or mother read the *Bhagavad Gita* to me during my junior and senior high school years: the text not only made sense, it was exciting. I wanted to bring that kind of excitement back into my classes and into the classes of other teachers of undergraduate students.

This desire to reach the general audience led me to do the present translation. To accomplish this task, I first translated the text of the *Bhagavad Gita* into a language with which the present-day undergraduate student is familiar, using simple words to capture the complex ideas of the text. To check and refine the translation, I utilized the editorial services of a bright undergraduate student with a major in English to strike out any difficult words that might be beyond the comprehension of students entering the first year of college.

Many generous people have contributed to the completion of this work. The idea of creating a new translation of the *Bhagavad Gita* was the brainchild of Maggie Barbieri at the Macmillan Publishing Company, who wanted a simple yet scholarly translation of the text to be a part of the Macmillan Library of Liberal Arts series. Since I was working on *Pathways to Philosophy* for Macmillan, which was to include my translation of a chapter from the *Bhagavad Gita*, Maggie asked me if I would do a translation of the entire text. I consented to do so. Maggie deserves my thanks for initiating the idea and offering all her assistance in the completion of this project. Rebecca Fisher, an undergraduate student from SUNY at Oneonta, offered her editorial assistance by going over the entire manuscript thoroughly, simplyfing words and sentences to meet the needs of present-day undergraduate students. Without her help and assistance the manuscript would not have been completed. I spent many hours with Dr. Shashikala Trivedi, a Sanskrit and *Bhagavad Gita* scholar from New Delhi, discussing the sanskrit text as well as the content of the *Bhagavad Gita*. I am indebted to her for being generous in spending her time and in offering crucial guidance. Thanks are due to Russell Blackwood of Hamilton College, John Koller of Rensselaer Polytechnic Institute, and Douglas Shrader of SUNY at Oneonta, who reviewed the entire manuscript and suggested some positive changes. I am grateful to Marjorie Holling, who typed this manuscript many times, always with an encouraging smile.

In the preparation of this translation, I have been guided by major translations of both Indian and Western scholars, to whom I am indebted.

Finally, I thank the editorial staff of Prentice Hall, and especially Angie Stone, for assistance and encouragement throughout the completion of this project.

Introduction

People interested in Indian philosophy are always asking, "Why do we need one more translation of the *Bhagavad Gita*? Especially since there are numerous translations already done by scholars, spiritual leaders, politicians, poets, and philosophers—aren't they enough?" *Bhagavad Gita* enthusiasts maintain that since the book has different meanings for different people, no single translation is capable of capturing the infinite number of semantic layers. Therefore, before I undertook this project, I asked myself the same question, "Why am I doing another translation?" I found that my answer was housed in my audience.

I have translated the *Bhagavad Gita* to reach undergraduate students and others who have not found the scholarly translations accessible. A large number of people who are not scholars, theologians, or academicians are still interested in reading the great works of mankind. To cater to this general readership, I have done this translation in a language that will reach a grassroots level audience. My translation is more of a *transcreation* because it deviates from the norm. It does not translate every word or phrase but still captures essential ideas and meanings that are crucial to the overall understanding of this great text. The impetus for my transcreation came from the life of Leo Tolstoy, who, after a voluminous production of great works of literature, came to the realization that he had been catering to the needs of a select few.

Tolstoy's works were read by the privileged cultural minority, which had been given everything by nature, society, and tradition. He realized that the masses of people who lived in cultural drudgery had a more genuine need for art than the privileged few. From then on, Tolstoy composed works that were intended to reach the ordinary people, whose passion for understanding the human predicament was as urgent, or more urgent, than that of the privileged few.

The *Bhagavad Gita* is not only a religious-philosophical work but also a great book of literature. It has appealed to the scholars in terms of its literary style and philosophical content; to the general practitioner, it has offered basic principles on how to live a meaningful life. Others still find it a mysterious book invoking an attraction-repulsion kind of fascination. My transcreation of the *Bhagavad Gita* is meant for all those students and readers who are curious about issues pertaining to the existential predicament of mankind. I present these themes in a language which will be easily understandable to the newly initiated.

Story Outline of the Bhagavad Gita

The *Bhagavad Gita* is a dialogue between Krishna and a warrior named Arjuna. It starts with a description of a war that is to be fought between the Pandavas and the Kauravas. These two families are related and both belong to a royal family in India. Arjuna and his four brothers make up the family of the Pandavas, whereas Duryodhana and his 99 brothers constitute the family of the Kauravas, which is headed by the blind king Dhritarashtra. Before the battle begins, Arjuna asks his charioteer Krishna to bring their chariot in between the two armies. As Arjuna glances on both sides, he sees his brothers, cousins, relatives, and teachers assembled to fight this war. When he reflects on this unusual situation, his determination to fight starts fading away, and his mind begins to fill up with uncertainty and doubt. He realizes that he is involved in an ethical dilemma. On one hand, his *duty as a warrior* is to safeguard the kingdom from external and internal dangers, while on the other hand, his *personal duty* dictates that he should protect his family and relatives from any physical injury. If he abides by the duty of a warrior, he must kill his relatives because they are evil, and yet, if he carries out his personal obligation, he must not fight the war. Since these two equally valid moralities are clashing within him, Arjuna is unable to decide. His mind is in turmoil. He challenges the morality of war by raising the following questions: Why is he fighting this war? What will he gain? What is the goal of victory? Is killing moral? Is war ever justified? Burdened by this confusion, Arjuna gets more and more doubtful and less and less sure of fighting. At the end of Chapter I, Arjuna puts down his bow and arrow and declares to Krishna that he is not going to fight.

In order to remove Arjuna's confusion, Krishna offers a number of convincing arguments for the justification of fighting this particular war. First, Krishna tells Arjuna that there is an immortal self called Atman that resides at the core of one's bodily self. Since this self is eternal, death happens only to the body.

Moreover, Krishna declares himself to be god who is the creator of the universe and all human beings. As a creator, Krishna assigns to each person a certain task and Arjuna is sent to this earth to eradicate the evil represented by the Kaurava brothers. Krishna tells Arjuna that he should fulfill his assigned duty by engaging in this war. Arjuna, who is guided by humanistic and pacifistic tendencies, is perplexed by Krishna's words. He is unconvinced by Krishna's reasoning about killing. When Krishna's logic does not work, he resorts to divine magic and reveals his cosmic form. Krishna tells Arjuna that he is not only speaking the truth, but that he *is* the truth. In the last chapter,

Arjuna's confusion is eradicated, and he is ready to fight the war as directed by Krishna.

The discourse between Krishna and Arjuna is spread out over eighteen chapters where the complete religious-philosophical system of Hinduism is presented. It covers such topics as the nature of the supreme being, the immortal self that resides in the human body, the four castes and their duties, the nature of the universe in terms of its material and conscious components, the different paths to self-realization, the relative and ultimate goals of life, and devotion to Krishna as the surest path to salvation.

Though the *Bhagavad Gita* is a dialogue between Arjuna and Krishna in which the former raises questions and the latter answers them, it is also a dialogue between the blind king, Dhritarashtra, and his minister, Sanjaya. After being unsuccessful in convincing his children (the Kauravas) and his nephews (the Pandavas) concerning the futility of war, the king decides to watch this gruesome event from the top of a close-by hill. Since he is blind, the sage Vyasa gives Sanjaya the intuitive vision which will enable him to witness the entire battle from a great distance and describe it to the king. The *Bhagavad Gita* opens with a question raised by Dhritarashtra and directed toward Sanjaya. The king wants to know what is going to happen on the battlefield. With the help of his intuitive vision, Sanjaya is able to describe the battle scene and the entire discourse between Krishna and Arjuna. The book concludes with Sanjaya reporting to King Dhritarashtra the excitement of listening to this glorious dialogue between Krishna and Arjuna, the rapturous delight of seeing the cosmic form of Krishna, and the expectation that wherever there is god Krishna and the great archer Arjuna, there will certainly be victory and glory.

Principal Characters

Arjuna   One of the Pandava princes. He is the great warrior who questions the reasons for fighting the war. His name means "silver white."

Bhima   One of the Pandava princes and brother of Arjuna. His name means "enormous" or "dreadful."

Bhishma   He is the grand uncle of the Panadavas. He has reluctantly chosen to fight the war. His name means "fearsome" or "shocking."

Dhritarashtra   The blind king whose children (the Kauravas) and nephews (the Pandavas) have gathered together to fight the war. His name means "he who controls the kingdom."

Duryodhana   Chief of the Kaurava princes. His name means "dirty fighter."

Drona   The great teacher who taught both the Kauravas and the Pandavas the art of war.

Krishna   The god-incarnate. Also, Arjuna's charioteer, who offers a metaphysical discourse which constitutes the text of the *Bhagavad Gita.*

Kauravas   The 100 sons of the blind king Dhritarashtra. They represent the forces of evil.

Pandavas   The five Pandava brothers: Yudhisthira, Bhima, Arjuna, Nakula, and Sahdeva. They represent the forces of good.

Sanjaya   He is the minister of King Dhristarashtra. Sanjaya is given the divine sight, by the sage Vyasa, through which he describes the battle to the blind king.

Transcreated Text of the *Bhagavad Gita*

Chapter I

Arjuna's Moral Dilemma

Summary:

The armies of Kauravas and Pandavas have assembled to fight a war. The blind king Dhritarashtra asks his minister, Sanjaya, to describe the battle and the dialogue between Arjuna, the Pandava warrior, and Krishna, the God incarnate, who is Arjuna's charioteer. Arjuna's chariot is brought between the two armies and he sees brothers, cousins, and relatives on both sides. He becomes unsure of fighting this war: to do his caste duty, he must fight his relatives; but to do his family duty, he must not kill them. He undergoes an ethical dilemma and refuses to fight.

Text:

◆ *Dhritarashtra[1] asked Sanjaya:[2]*

Tell me about my children and Pandava's children, who have assembled in the field of righteousness to fight a battle.   1:1

◆ *Sanjaya replied:*

After scrutinizing the army of the Pandavas, Duryodhana[3] came closer to his teacher, Drona,[4] and said: 1:2

---

[1]Dhritarashtra is the blind king, whose children (the Kauravas) and nephews (the Pandavas) have gathered together to fight this war.

[2]The minister of Dhritarashtra has been given Divine Sight by the sage Vyasa so that he could describe the entire battle to the blind king.

[3]Duryodhana is the chief of the Kaurava princes. His name means "dirty fighter."

[4]The great teacher who taught both the Kauravas and the Pandavas the art of war.

"Behold the Pandavas' huge army arranged by the intelligent son of Drupada.   1:3

In *their* army there are great archers like Arjuna, Bhima, Yayudhana, Virata, and the mighty charioteer Drupada.   1:4

Dhrishtaketu, Cekitana, and the mighty king of Varanasi; Purujit, Kuntibhoja, and Saibya, who are the best among men.   1:5

The performer of great deeds, Yudhamanyu, the bold Uttamauja, Abhimanyu, and Draupadi's sons, are all great charioteers.   1:6

O Drona, great among the brahmins! Now I will tell you the names of *our* mighty soldiers and commanders.   1:7

Your revered self, Bhishma, Karna, the victorious Kripa, Ashvatthama, Vikarna, and the son of Somadatta.   1:8

Not only are they skilled in weaponry and in the art of warfare, but they are also ready to sacrifice their lives for me.   1:9

Bhishma is the defender of our limitless and undefeatable army, whereas Bhima is the defender of the limited and defeatable army of the Pandavas."   1:10

Then Duryodhana commanded his army, "All of you take your posts and cautiously safeguard our commander-in-chief Bhishma."   1:11

To make Duryodhana happy, Bhishma blew his mighty conch hard, like a lion's roar.   1:12

The conches, kettledrums, horns, and tabors resounded together producing a horrifying sound.   1:13

While sitting in their chariot with white horses, Krishna and Arjuna of the other army blew their godly conches.   1:14

Krishna blew *pancajanya* (acquired from a demon), Arjuna, *devadatta* (bestowed by the gods), and Bhima, *paundra* (powerful conch).   1:15

King Yudhisthira, the son of Kunti, blew *anantavijaya* (eternal victory), while Nukula and Sahdeva blew *sughosa* (sweet tone) and *manipuspaka* (jewel flower).   1:16

The skillful archer, the king of Varanasi, the mighty charioteer-fighter Shikhandin, Dhrishtadyumna, Virata, and the undefeatable Satyaki,   1:17

The King Drupada, Draupadi's five sons, and the strong-armed Abhimanyu, blew their conches one by one.   1:18

The thunderous sound of the conches shook the earth, the sky, and the confidence of Dhritarashtra's army.   1:19

◆ *Sanjaya continued his explanation:*

Just when the battle was about to start and Dhritarashtra's children were ready to fight, Arjuna picked up his bow and turned to Krishna.   1:20

Arjuna said, "Bring my chariot in between the two armies!   1:21

I wish to see the ones who are desirous of this war.   1:22

I want to look at all of those who are supporting the misguided Duryodhana."   1:23

As directed by Arjuna, Krishna brought the shining chariot in the middle of the two armies.   1:24

Glancing directly toward Bhishma, Drona, and the powerful kings, Krishna said, "Arjuna, look at the Kauravas with your own eyes."   1:25

Arjuna saw his uncles, grandfathers, teachers, brothers, sons, grandsons, and friends in the two armies.   1:26

Seeing his fathers-in-laws, friends, and relatives assembled for war, Arjuna was overcome with great compassion and said to Krishna: 1:27

"On seeing my relatives who are desirous of fighting this war, my limbs have become numb, my throat has turned dry, my body is trembling, and my hair is standing on end.   1:28,29

My skin is burning, my mind is confused, I can't stand up straight, and the mighty bow[5] is falling out of my sweaty hands.   1:30

I see unholy omens. This fight seems illogical and unnecessary. Nothing good will come out of killing my own relatives.   1:31

Glory, happiness, or victory are no use to me. I do not desire a kingdom, pleasures, or life.   1:32

Those who seek a kingdom, pleasures, and enjoyments are assembled here to fight a battle for which they have put their lives and property at stake.   1:33

There are teachers, fathers, sons, grandfathers, maternal uncles, fathers-in-laws, grandsons, brothers-in-laws, and other relatives all fighting against each other.   1:34

The kingdom of the earth and the *three worlds*[6] is not worth killing them. I would rather let them take my life instead.   1:35

What is the benefit of killing the sons of Dhritarashtra? By slaughtering our ignoble kin, we can only accumulate sin.   1:36

---

[5]The "mighty bow" is a translation of the Sanskrit word *gandiva*.

[6]The Sanskrit word is *Trialokya*, which refers to the *"three worlds"* of the earthly, atmospheric, and heavenly beings.

For this reason, I shall not kill my relatives. It is below me to kill my kinsmen because there is no happiness in this kind of act.   1:37

Blinded by greed, these people do not see any sin in the destruction of their own clan or in the hatred of their friends.   1:38

Those of us who have the clarity of mind to discern right from wrong ought to stay away from the destruction of our family.   1:39

With the destruction of the family, the ancient traditions would perish, and when tradition is destroyed lawlessness will increase.   1:40

With the growth of lawlessness, the women of the family will be corrupted; and if they go astray, the caste system will get mixed up.   1:41

The mixing of castes sounds a death knell for all families because therein respect for the ancestors is lost.   1:42

Through their wrongdoings, the corrupters of the family would create caste confusion and thus both the caste duties and the traditional laws of the family would be destroyed.   1:43

O Krishna, it is common knowledge that when family tradition disappears, the relatives secure their place in hell.   1:44

I was ready to kill my own relatives and covet the kingdom, and through that, I was going to perform a terrible deed.   1:45

If the sons of Dhritarashtra, armed with weapons, kill me while I am unarmed and unresisting in the field of battle, I will happily find my salvation."   1:46

Overwhelmed by grief, Arjuna placed aside his bow and arrows and sat down in the chariot.   1:47

Chapter II

Path of Knowledge

Summary:

Arjuna is downhearted and discouraged. He doesn't want to kill his revered teachers and relatives. Because his mind is confused, he wants Krishna to remove this doubt through knowledge. In order to lift up Arjuna's spirits, Krishna tells him that the wise do not grieve. They know the nature of the real self, called Atman. This self is immortal and resides at the core of one's being. Death happens only to the body and not to Atman. As a creator, Krishna assigns to each person a certain task, and Arjuna is sent to this earth to eradicate the evil represented by the Kauravas. By killing these warriors, Arjuna would only be destroying their bodies and not their Atman. Krishna tells Arjuna that he ought to be unwavering in the performance of his duty—he should become focused and fight.

Text:

◆ *Krishna spoke to Arjuna*—who was engulfed in self-pity, whose eyes were filled with tears, and whose heart was laden with grief—*the following words:*   2:1

During this crises, your faintheartedness is disgraceful. At the moment, you are not acting like a warrior, and this is hurting your chances of heavenly fulfillment.   2:2

Do not take the path of cowardice. It benefits you in no way. Get rid of this weakness in your heart and prepare yourself for battle.   2:3

◆ *Arjuna responded:*

How could I attack my venerable teachers like Bhishma and Drona? How could I hurt them?   2:4

In this world, it is better to eat bread obtained through begging than to kill these great teachers. One who kills his teachers for the sake of wealth eats food stained by blood.   2:5

We do not know who will be victorious in this battle. Even if we gain victory over the sons of Dhritarashtra (who oppose us), we would be killing those who give us a reason to live.   2:6

O Krishna, pity has destroyed my discernment and doubt has ensnared my sense of duty. I entreat you to show me the right path. As a disciple, I have come·to sit at your feet to gain knowledge from you.   2:7

Even if I obtain unrivaled control over the kingdom of earth or sovereignty over the gods, I don't see any way to ease the sorrow that is numbing my senses.   2:8

◆ *Sanjaya continued:*

After exclaiming, "I will not fight, Krishna," Arjuna became silent. 2:9

While the grief stricken Arjuna sat in the middle of the two armies, Krishna said to him: 2:10

Do you think you are being wise by grieving for those who do not deserve grieving? The wise do not mourn the living or the dead.   2:11

It is impossible that there was ever a time when neither I, nor you, nor the kings were not, and there never will be a time when all of us will cease to be.   2:12

The inner self (Atman),[7] while dwelling in the body, undergoes the experiences of childhood, youth, and old age. Similarly, it also moves on from one body to the next at death. The wise do not doubt this knowledge.   2:13

The sensations of hot, cold, pain, and pleasure are caused by contact between the body and objects. Since these feelings are transient, learn to endure them, Arjuna.   2:14

One who remains steadfast in pleasure and pain and is not distracted by sensations is a person worthy of eternal fulfillment.   2:15

The nonexistent never comes into being and the existent does not ever cease to be. The sages who clearly distinguish this fact are the discerners of truth.   2:16

---

[7]The word *Atman* is used for the spark of divinity that resides at the core of our physical and mental being. Since no single English translation conveys its full meaning, I will be using such words as consciousness, inner self, divine self, and divine spark to capture the nuances of its meaning.

The self that permeates the manifest world is indestructible. No one can destroy this immutable reality. 2:17

Since only the bodies pervaded by this indestructible, immeasurable, and immutable self are prone to destruction, you must prepare yourself to fight. 2:18

Those who think that this divine self is the slayer or the slain are far from the truth because this self does not slay nor is it slain. 2:19

This divine self is not born and it does not die. It never came into being and will not ever cease to be. This self is unborn, eternal, unchanging, and immutable. It does not die even when the body ceases to be. 2:20

How can one, who knows this self to be eternal, indestructible, and birthless, kill anyone or cause anyone to kill? 2:21

Just as a person discards the worn-out clothes and puts on the new ones, similarly the self discards the old body and enters into a new one. 2:22

This self cannot be cut by weapons, burnt by fire, soaked by water, or dried by wind. 2:23

This self, which cannot be pierced, burnt, wetted or withered, is eternal, all-permeating, changeless, and immutable. 2:24

Know this self to be unmanifest, indescribable, and everlasting. Therefore, do not grieve, Arjuna. 2:25

Even if you believe that this self undergoes repeated births and deaths, you should still not grieve. 2:26

One who is born is sure to die and one who is dead is certain to be born. It is therefore futile to mourn that which is inevitable. 2:27

All beings are unmanifest before birth, manifest after birth, and unmanifest again after death. Do not indulge in unnecessary sorrow. 2:28

Though one marvels this self through seeing, describing, and listening, yet one does not have knowledge of it. 2:29

Arjuna, you should know that since the divine self pervades all beings, there is no reason for you to be troubled. 2:30

Keeping your duty in mind, you should not be confused because a warrior should look forward to fighting a righteous war. 2:31

Lucky are the warriors who get this opportunity to fight a war that by its own accord will lead them to heaven. 2:32

If you refuse to fight this righteous battle you will go against your duty, your honor will be diminished, and your moral self worth will be lowered. 2:33

You will beget ill-fame, which for an honorable person is worse than death. 2:34

The chariot-warriors will think that you ran away from fighting a battle out of fear. Those who had held you in high esteem will look down upon you.   2:35

Your enemies will slander your name and speak ill of you. What could be more disturbing than that?   2:36

If you are killed in the battle, you will earn a place in heaven; if you are victorious, you will enjoy the kingdom of this earth; therefore, arise and fight this battle with all of your might.   2:37

By treating both pain and pleasure, gain and loss, victory and defeat equally, and by preparing to fight the battle, you will not incur any moral blame.   2:38

Arjuna, I have described to you the path of knowledge. Now listen to its practical side, which will lead you to salvation.   2:39

When you follow this path, effort is not wasted and failure is not encountered. Even a few footsteps in the right direction will release you from fear.   2:40

The will of the follower of this path is focused, whereas the one whose will lacks this clarity is directed toward many goals.   2:41

The unwise who take delight in rhetoric and believe in the letter of the *Vedas*[8] think of their way as the only way.   2:42

While striving toward the heavenly abode, the ignorant ones are preoccupied with self-gratification. They indulge in many rituals that will determine their rebirth in the next life.   2:43

The ignorant who are attached to pleasure and power, and whose discrimination is effaced are incapable of achieving inner focus.   2:44

Transcend the three qualities[9] that constitute the province of the *Vedas*. Develop indifference toward dichotomy. Be steadfast in tranquility. Discard the tendency toward hoarding and selfish craving. Center your mind on the inner self.   2:45

When the flood water covers the land, the reservoir becomes useless. Similarly, for an enlightened sage the Vedic knowledge serves no function.   2:46

You have an obligation to perform an action but no right to its fruits. Work without any motive for reward; but never shrink from work.   2:47

[8]The *Vedas* are the four earliest philosophical–religious books of the Hindus. They emphasize rituals to gain access to gods and goddesses.

[9]The word "qualities" is used for the term *gunas*. All material objects, including human bodies, are constructed from *gunas*.

Perform your action by focusing your mind; abandon all attachments; transcend both success and failure. This evenness of mind is called yoga.[10]   2:48

An action performed for a reward is inferior to one performed for its own sake. Take refuge in a focused mind. Those who seek remuneration are unfortunate.   2:49

One who has achieved a focused mind transcends both good and evil. Strive for mental focus because it is perfection in action.   2:50

Those with a clear mind, having freed themselves from needing rewards for their actions and from believing in the fetters of births, are able to attain a sorrowless state.   2:51

When one's understanding is clear and beyond the darkness of ignorance, one becomes oblivious to the knowledge of the scriptures.   2:52

Unperturbed by the teachings of the sacred scriptures and having achieved a tranquil mind, one becomes a perfect sage.   2:53

◆ *Arjuna inquired:*

How would you describe a perfect sage? How would this person speak, sit, or walk?   2:54

◆ *Krishna replied:*

A perfect sage is one who has transcended all of his desires and is totally content with himself.   2:55

He who is unperturbed by misfortune, has extinguished the desire for pleasure, has erased passion, fear, and rage, is a perfect sage. 2:56

He who has no attachment to anyone and is neither happy nor sad in the attainment of evil, fortune, or misfortune, is a perfect sage.   2:57

A perfect sage is able to withdraw his mind completely from the objects of sense like a turtle that can retract its limbs into its shell. 2:58

He who turns away from the objects of sense still has a desire for them. But when he experiences the highest self, even this desire finally disappears.   2:59

The power of senses is so great that it may drive the seeker of perfection away from his goal.   2:60

---

[10]Yoga means "union," and more specifically refers to a system of philosophy that was started in 500 BC. As a method, it helps the initiate to realize the union between oneself and the divine self.

He who has mastered his senses then totally focuses his attention on me. When these senses are subjugated, a man's wisdom is firmly established.   2:61

Through his involvement with objects, he gets attracted to them; this attraction arouses desire, and the unfulfillment of desire produces anger.   2:62

Anger gives rise to bewilderment; bewilderment erases memory; loss of memory destroys the spirit, and with the destruction of spirit a person perishes.   2:63

When a man takes delight in the engagement of his senses with objects and is neither attracted nor repelled by them, and has attained complete mastery over his mind, he achieves absolute serenity.   2:64

He who obtains this serenity is devoid of all sorrow. This tranquil state brings about total mental equilibrium.   2:65

On the other hand, he who has no control, has no focus and no power of concentration. Lack of concentration leads to deprivation of peace and without peace there is no happiness.   2:66

He whose mind is swayed by the senses is like a ship that is carried away to different waters by uncontrolled winds.   2:67

O mighty-armed Arjuna, those whose senses are fully controlled and held in check from objects are securely grounded.   2:68

He who has wisdom is awake when others are asleep, and such a person is asleep when others are awake.   2:69

A man with established wisdom lets all desires enter his being. Yet, this man is tranquil like an ocean into which all the rivers flow, and though it gets filled up, remains unmoving. In contrast, he who is driven by desires never finds peace.   2:70

Thus, he who renounces all desires and is free of cravings and egoism attains total serenity.   2:71

This is the supreme state. A person who achieves it is able to erase his misperceptions of reality. At the time of death, this person will attain an ecstatic union with the divine self.   2:72

Chapter III

Path of Action

Summary:

Arjuna asks Krishna why he should fight in this terrible war if action is inferior to knowledge as a path to the divine self. Krishna tells Arjuna that there are two paths of salvation. The path of knowledge is for the wise, whereas the path of work is for the man of action. No one ever reaches perfection through inaction or renunciation. Since Arjuna is a man of action, he should grasp the nature of action. Because everything is created, supported, and destroyed by action, according to Krishna, action permeates all aspects of life and existence. An action leads to salvation when performed with controlled senses, with detachment, with devotion, with full involvement, and with selflessness. An action that is carried out as a duty and without the desire for beneficial consequences is superior. To fight this war is Arjuna's preordained obligation; Krishna urges him, therefore, to put all of his energies into performing his duty unselfishly.

Text:

◆ *Arjuna spoke to Krishna:*

If you regard the path of knowledge to be superior to the path of action, why do you insist that I should perform such a horrible deed?   3:1

Your conflicting statements are confusing my mind. Give me a definitive answer regarding the path through which I may reach the divine self.
3:2

◆ *Krishna replied to Arjuna:*

As I told you earlier, there are two paths of salvation open to the people of this world. The path of knowledge is for people of wisdom and the path of work is for people of action.   3:3

Perfection cannot be reached either through inaction or renunciation of work.   3:4

No human being can stay inactive even for a moment. Since nature endows everyone with certain qualities, each person is propelled to work continuously.   3:5

He who controls his actions in order to reach toward the divine self while still being driven by the senses is a hypocrite.   3:6

But he whose mind is in control of the senses and who performs actions without attachment is a superior person.   3:7

Keep performing your assigned duties, Arjuna, because action is better than nonaction. Even the body needs to remain working in order to sustain itself.   3:8

This world is bound by actions except those performed in the spirit of worship. Therefore, Arjuna, let your actions be selfless and performed in the spirit of worship.   3:9

At the time of the creation of the universe and human beings, the creator said, "Multiply yourself through action performed in the spirit of worship. Let this universe be your wish-fulfilling cow."[11]   3:10

You should honor the gods through worship and the gods will cherish you in return. Through this mutual respect, you will reach the divine self.   3:11

When gods are honored with worship, they will bestow on you the satisfaction of your desires. A person is a thief who takes these god-given gifts without giving anything in return.   3:12

Those who eat food sanctified by worship are freed from evil, whereas those who cook selfishly for themselves eat tainted food.   3:13

Life is born out of food; food is produced by rain; rain is caused by sacrifice, and sacrifice is due to action.   3:14

Action originates in prayer,[12] which depends on the sound *Om,* the concrete expression of the imperishable; and the imperishable persists in all acts of sacrifice.   3:15

He who does not grasp this cycle of change, but lives engrossed in the malicious delight of his senses, lives life in vain.   3:16

He who takes pleasure in the inner self, is content with the inner self, and is focused on the inner self, has no task left to be performed.   3:17

This person has nothing to profit from actions performed in the past or yet to be performed in the future, and has nothing to gain from others.   3:18

---

[11]The wish-fulfilling cow is a Hindu mythological creature that possesses a woman's head, a cow's body, and a bird's wings. It fulfills all the desires and wants of whosoever owns it.

[12]The word *brahmana* is used in the *Vedas* to refer to "prayer" or "infinite creative spirit." Here I am translating it as prayer because it conveys the intended meaning.

Therefore, Arjuna, perform your duty unselfishly. By so doing, you will reach the abode of the divine self. 3:19

King Janaka[13] and others reached perfection by performing these kinds of actions. Let your actions be performed in this spirit and with the intention of helping mankind. 3:20

A noble person performs exemplary acts that then become a model for others to follow. 3:21

There is nothing that I have yet to do, nor anything that I have to attain, yet I keep on working. 3:22

For if I ever stop working, those who follow my example will do the same. 3:23

If for a single moment I stop working, the world will perish, chaos will follow, and all creatures will be destroyed. 3:24

The unwise indulge in selfish work for personal gain, whereas the wise indulge in unselfish work for the benefit of humanity. 3:25

The wise should not create confusion in the minds of the unwise who are attached to action. Instead, the wise should perform action unselfishly to set an example for the unwise. 3:26

Though all actions are performed by qualities[14] embedded in one's nature, he who is deluded by his ego believes "I am the doer." 3:27

He who can discern the difference between qualities and actions knows that senses are interacting with other senses, and he is thereby detached from action. 3:28

Those who are confused by qualities get attached to the results produced by them. But those who have complete knowledge of this reality should not cause conflict in the ignorant ones, who only possess partial knowledge. 3:29

By focusing your mind on the inner self—surrendering all actions to me, freeing yourself from selfish desire, and delivering yourself from the fever of anxiety—you get ready to fight. 3:30

Those who devote themselves to my teaching without finding any flaws in it and live according to its dictates are freed from the bondage of their actions. 3:31

And those who look down upon my teaching and shun its practice will be deprived of this wisdom and are surely doomed. 3:32

---

[13]King Janaka is a legendary Hindu king who administered his realm by performing unselfish actions for the benefit of the kingdom as a whole.

[14]The word "qualities" is used for the term *gunas*.

All men, including the wise, act according to their natures. What will self-control accomplish?   3:33

There is a natural attraction and repulsion between the senses and their objects. Do not be trapped by these two ensnarers.   3:34

It is better to perform one's own duty imperfectly than to perform another's perfectly. To die performing one's own duty is better, since the performance of another's duty is precarious.   3:35

◆ *Arjuna inquired further:*

Tell me Krishna, why does a person unintentionally do bad deeds? 3:36

◆ *Krishna replied:*

All-consuming desire and anger arise from passion. They are your enemies.   3:37

Just as smoke can smother a fire, dust can cover a mirror, and a womb can envelop an embryo—desire can cover wisdom.   3:38

This insatiable desire, which is the eternal enemy of the wise, keeps their knowledge entrapped.   3:39

This fire of desire works through the senses, the mind, and the intellect. By constraining wisdom, it keeps the person away from the knowledge of the inner self.   3:40

O Arjuna, discipline your senses and destroy this enemy of wisdom. 3:41

It is said that senses are powerful; more powerful than the senses is the mind. More powerful than the mind is the intellect, and more powerful than the intellect is the inner self.   3:42

Thus, knowing the inner self to be superior to the intellect, arise and kill this fire of desire, which is your real enemy.   3:43

Chapter IV

Paths of Action and Knowledge

Summary:

Krishna wants to teach Arjuna an ancient wisdom that has been passed down from the gods to the sages and then to human devotees. There are two parts to this wisdom. First, Krishna tells Arjuna that he is an incarnation of Vishnu—the preserver of the universe. Whenever evil increases, Krishna takes material form to come down to earth to help the good forces to eradicate the evildoers. He has come in the form of Krishna to help Arjuna to destroy the evil Kauravas. Second, Krishna makes a distinction between action, wrong action, and nonaction. An action motivated by the desire for rewards irrespective of its injurious consequences for oneself or others is a wrong action. In contrast, any action performed spontaneously and without any desire for rewards is a good action. Krishna describes a good action as desireless and purified by insight, performed spontaneously and with contentment, carried out with a disciplined mind and heart, and as an offering to the divine self. One who executes an action while being guided by the knowledge of these qualities achieves nonaction in action.

Text:

◆ *Krishna spoke further:*

I conveyed this wisdom to the luminous sun[15] who related it to his son, Manu,[16] the progenitor, and Manu transmitted it to his son, the solar king.[17]   4:1

The royal sages knew this tradition of transmission of wisdom, but as time passed, this wisdom was forgotten.   4:2

The same ancient wisdom is being conveyed today to you by me because you are my devotee and companion.   4:3

[15]Vivasvat is the sun, which is the giver of light.

[16]Hindus regard Manu as the parent of the human race.

[17]Iksvaku is the son of Manu, who is regarded as the solar king.

◆ *Arjuna questioned Krishna:*

You were born recently, but the sun was born a long time ago. How can I believe that you imparted this wisdom to the sun?   4:4

◆ *Krishna replied:*

I and you have been born many times. I know it, but you have forgotten it.   4:5

Though I am unborn, eternal and Lord of all creatures, I take birth on this earth through my power of divine playfulness.[18]   4:6

Whenever righteousness decreases and unrighteousness flourishes, I am born on this earth to restore the balance.   4:7

I am born throughout different ages to protect the sages, to destroy the evildoers, and to establish righteousness.   4:8

Those who have knowledge of my divine birth and actions, at the time of their death, are not reborn but instead return to me.   4:9

Those who have discarded desire, fear, and anger, and have purified themselves through the austerity of wisdom are absorbed in me. By taking shelter in me, they have attained me by becoming me.   4:10

I reward people according to the way they offer their worship to me. Whatever path people may follow, they all follow my path.   4:11

People offer worship to gods to earn rewards because good deeds result in quick beneficial consequences on this earth.   4:12

I have created the four castes according to man's natural predispositions and actions. Though I am their author, I am eternally beyond action. 4:13

I am not bound by my actions nor any fruits of action. He who understands me in this way is also free from his actions.   4:14

The ancient sages who sought perfection were guided by this wisdom. So Arjuna, in the performance of your actions, follow their example.   4:15

Even the scholars are confused about action and nonaction. I will distinguish these two for you. Once you understand this, you will be free from confusion and attain wisdom.   4:16

Since the nature of action is complex, it is important to learn the distinction between action, wrong action,[19] and nonaction.   4:17

A man is wise who sees *nonaction in action* and *action in nonaction*. Such a person is disciplined in his deeds.   4:18

---

[18]*Lila* is "divine playfulness," through which the universe is created.

[19]A detailed discussion of action is presented in Chapters XVI and XVII.

He who performs desireless actions and is purified by insight is regarded by the wise to be learned. 4:19

Nonaction in action involves contentment, spontaneity, nonexertion, and detachment from beneficial consequences. 4:20

He who is devoid of expectations, whose heart and mind are disciplined, and who lets the body act spontaneously is above any moral blemish. 4:21

A person is not bound by his actions when he is devoid of envy and is equable toward success or failure. 4:22

All those actions which are free from desire, grounded by wisdom, imbued with devotion, and performed without expectations are regarded as pure acts. 4:23

He who identifies worship and offerings with the inner self and performs all actions, being engrossed in the inner self, reaches the inner self. 4:24

Some sages offer worship to the deities, whereas others offer their self as a sacrifice to the fire of the inner self. 4:25

Some sages offer the sacrifice of their senses, whereas the others offer the objects of their senses as homage. 4:26

And yet others offer all the actions of their senses and those of their vital breath into the fire of self-restraint ignited by wisdom. 4:27

While some offer wealth, austerities, and rituals, those with a disciplined mind offer learning and wisdom. 4:28

Those who are interested in the control of the vital breath[20] offer the process of inhalation, retention, and exhalation as a sacrifice. 4:29

Others, who have learned to control their life force[21] through restricted food intake, offer this vital force as a sacrifice. 4:30

Those who enjoy the elixir of the sacrificial remnants join the inner self. Those who don't sacrifice will not find enjoyment in this or any higher world. 4:31

These and many other forms of worship are described in the holy scriptures. He who knows them will gain freedom. 4:32

Though the goal of action is wisdom, the offering of knowledge has greater importance than the sacrifice of wealth. 4:33

The seers of truth can teach you this wisdom. Bow devotedly before them, ask them questions and attend to them. 4:34

---

[20]*Pranayama* or "the control of breathing" or "life force." It is one of the steps in the yoga method.

[21]This refers to *prana* or vital force, which is needed for the proper functioning of the body and mind.

O Arjuna, once you grasp this truth, you will have no confusion. You will see all creation in yourself and me.   4:35

The worst evildoer can swim over the river of evil with a raft of wisdom.   4:36

Like the fire that consumes the wood and turns it into ashes, so does wisdom reduce action to ashes.   4:37

Wisdom is the highest purifier in this world. He who has gained control over himself will realize this purity in due time.   4:38

He who has developed faith and control over his senses gains wisdom, which in turn leads him quickly toward complete peace of mind.   4:39

On the other hand, an unwise man who is without faith or is full of doubts destroys himself.   4:40

He who has disciplined his actions, has eliminated doubt through knowledge, and has taken shelter in the inner self is not bound by actions.   4:41

O Arjuna, this doubt that dwells in your heart is born out of ignorance. Slay this doubt with the sword of wisdom and arise.   4:42

Chapter V

Path of Renunciation

Summary:

After informing Arjuna that action is preferable to renunciation, Krishna offers a detailed description of renunciation. Krishna points out that a wise man does not distinguish between action and renunciation. A true renunciate is above love and hate, attachment and repulsion, and one who has subdued the body and the mind. Such a person lets the body, intellect, and mind perform their functions naturally and spontaneously. This person is unattached to all actions or their rewards. The nature of renunciation consists of effortless performance of an action in the spirit of worship to the divine self.

Text:

◆ *Arjuna asked Krishna:*

First you say that a man should renounce action, and then you praise the performance of action—please tell me exactly which one of the two is better.   5:1

◆ *Krishna replied:*

Though action and renunciation of action are equally conducive to salvation, action is better.   5:2

He who has perfected renunciation neither hates anyone nor desires anything. Such a person is disentangled from the clutches of the world.   5:3

The foolish distinguish between the paths of action and renunciation, whereas the wise do not. A man who perfects either one of them enjoys the benefits of both.   5:4

Those established in the path of renunciation have the same status as those established in the path of action. He who grasps this identity understands an important truth.   5:5

Without disciplined action, a man cannot attain renunciation. But with disciplined action, a sage reaches the inner self with ease.   5:6

A man with a pure heart who has complete control over the senses, who is disciplined in action, and who identifies with all other creatures is not tainted by action.   5:7

While seeing, hearing, smelling, eating, walking, and breathing, a man of disciplined action who knows reality reminds himself that he is doing nothing.   5:8

While speaking, giving, and taking, the senses are engaged in their activities and the knower of reality does nothing that involves effort.   5:9

Like the lotus flower that is untouched by dirty water, a man absorbed in the inner self who relinquishes the action is untainted by any moral blemish.   5:10

When completely unattached, a disciplined man uses the body, the heart, the mind, and the senses toward purifying the inner self.   5:11

A disciplined man abandons the fruits of his action and attains unlimited peace, but an undisciplined man becomes a slave to the rewards of his action.   5:12

He who has mentally detached himself from all actions, neither doing anything himself nor forcing others to do anything, dwells happily in a body of nine gates.[22]   5:13

The inner self is not the doer, the cause or the fruit of action. The physical nature of a human being is responsible for these.   5:14

The inner self cannot take upon itself the merits or demerits of a man. Since ignorance envelops knowledge, a human being is inherently misled.   5:15

But just as the sun illuminates the nature of the world with its light, so do others who destroy their ignorance with the aid of wisdom display the form of the supreme being.   5:16

He whose intellect resides in the supreme being, whose heart is engrossed in it, who makes it the ultimate goal of life and the only object of worship, frees himself from the birth–death cycle.   5:17

A wise man makes no distinction between a scholar, a cow, a dog, an elephant, or an outcast.   5:18

Men whose hearts are imbued with this sense of equality are able to overcome the birth–death cycle of this world. They find repose in the supreme being who is flawless and is present in everything.   5:19

---

[22]This refers to the nine openings of the human body: the two eyes, two ears, two nostrils, the mouth, the anus, and the genital organ.

He who resides in the supreme being possesses a stable intelligence totally free from attachment, and is neither happy for obtaining something pleasant nor unhappy for obtaining something unpleasant.   5:20

When a man is not attracted to external objects, he finds peace at the core of his being. When he is totally absorbed in the contemplation of the supreme being, he finds unlimited happiness.   5:21

The pleasure that a man obtains through contact with objects is actually the source of sorrow because it is impermanent. O Arjuna, wise men are uninterested in it.   5:22

By successfully controlling anger and desire, a man may find true happiness in this life.   5:23

A man who finds peace, bliss, and the spark of divinity within is absorbed into the supreme being and thus becomes this being.   5:24

Those whose bad deeds are destroyed, whose uncertainties are eradicated, whose hearts are disciplined, and who take delight in helping all creatures are sages who have achieved liberation.   5:25

He who is free of desire and anger, is in control of his heart, and who has knowledge of the supreme self within, achieves the eternal peace of the supreme being.   5:26

By cutting off his contact with external objects, by focusing vision between the eyebrows, by regulating the inhalation and exhalation of breath, and by controlling the sense organs, heart, and mind, he who has become oblivious to desire, fear, and anger has obtained true freedom.   5:27,28

He who regards me as the receiver of all sacrifice and prayer, controller of the entire universe, and friend of all creatures, attains peace.   5:29

Chapter VI

The Nature of a True Yogi

Summary:

Krishna describes the method of yoga as well as the nature of a yogi, one who is accomplished in this method. A true yogi is a person of action. Like the renunciate, a yogi is detached from the objects of senses, from the rewards of actions, and from all desires. Furthermore, a yogi achieves total control over his nature and attains serenity. Stability in knowledge, equilibrium of mind, detachment from material things, treating friends and adversaries alike, being impartial toward saints and sinners, and being continuously involved in yoga practices are the distinguishing marks of a yogi. On the other hand, the method of yoga involves such practices as retreating to a solitary spot, living alone, discarding material possessions, and sitting in a lotus posture with the body, head, and neck erect and steady, focusing on the tip of one's nose, and meditating on the divine self. He who has perfected the method of yoga is a true yogi. Krishna says, "O Arjuna, since a true yogi is superior to the ascetic, the learned, or the performer of rituals, be a yogi."

Text:

◆ *Krishna spoke:*

He who performs his duty without seeking any reward is a yogi. The one who fails to work or neglects to indulge in religious obligations is not.   6:1

A true yogi is a man of action. No man can be so unless he can discard all desires.   6:2

A sage who wants to be a yogi follows the path of action. Once this stage is reached, he follows the path of serenity.   6:3

A man becomes a yogi when attraction to sense objects, to rewards, and to desires ceases to exist.   6:4

A man should not degrade himself. Rather, he should raise the self through oneself, because a man is his own friend or enemy.   6:5

He who has disciplined himself has befriended the inner self. He who has not subdued his nature has made the inner self as his enemy.   6:6

When a man has achieved total control over his nature and has attained serenity, his inner self remains calm in heat or cold, during happiness or unhappiness, and in honor or dishonor.   6:7

A man is a true yogi who is stable in knowledge and wisdom, who has attained equilibrium and has controlled all the five senses. Such a person makes no distinction between a lump of clay, a stone, or a piece of gold.   6:8

He who treats friends, companions, and adversaries alike, who is neutral toward enemies and kinsmen and is impartial toward saints and sinners is an exemplary person.   6:9

A true yogi should find a solitary retreat, stay alone, control his senses, and discard all possessions while remaining fully focused on the inner self.   6:10

A yogi should find a firm seat that is neither too high nor too low and is covered by a cloth, deer skin, or grass.   6:11

By sitting steadily, focusing his mind on a single object, and keeping thoughts and senses under control, a yogi should practice yoga for the sake of purification of the self.   6:12

A yogi should keep his body, head, and neck erect while looking at the tip of the nose with steady eyes.   6:13

Being firmly established in chastity, with calmness, fearlessness, and a disciplined mind, a yogi should sit focused and fully absorbed in me.   6:14

A yogi, whose mind is fully controlled and who is continuously involved in yoga practices, attains the supreme peace that resides in my nature.   6:15

O Arjuna, he who eats a lot or fasts a great deal, or sleeps too much or too little, cannot achieve the yogic state.   6:16

Yoga helps destroy the sorrow of anyone who is moderate in eating and recreation or sleeping and working.   6:17

He whose subdued mind dwells in the self and is freed of desires and cravings is said to have become a true yogi.   6:18

Just as a lamp does not flicker in a windless place, the disciplined mind of a yogi doesn't waver in the peaceful contemplation of the inner self. 6:19

A man who develops control over his mind through the practice of yoga, and who displays the inner self through his deeds, takes delight in the inner self.   6:20

Supreme bliss, which is beyond the grasp of senses and yet can be comprehended by intelligence, is a truth which a yogi knows and firmly holds onto it.   6:21

And having achieved this indescribable state, a yogi is unshaken by any sorrow.   6:22

By grasping this separation from sorrow, a yogi should undertake discipline with complete determination and firmness of heart.   6:23

A yogi should transcend all desires rooted in passions and should control all senses with the mind.   6:24

A yogi whose mind is completely focused on the self and is undisturbed should gradually develop tranquility.   6:25

An unsteady and wandering mind can be made steady and restful through self-discipline.   6:26

A yogi will experience supreme happiness when he has calmed the mind, pacified his passions, and identified himself with the inner self.   6:27

When a yogi is united with the inner self, he will transcend imperfection and reach supernal bliss.   6:28

A yogi whose mind has become focused through yoga sees the inner self in all creatures and all creatures within the inner self.   6:29

And he who sees me in all things and all things in me is never separated from me, nor am I separated from such a person.   6:30

Whichever way one acts, a person who is focused and worships me as being present in all creatures will always reside in me.   6:31

O Arjuna, he who is empathetic to the pains and pleasures of all creatures is a yogi of the highest order.   6:32

◆ *Arjuna replied:*

Since my mind is restless, its stillness through yoga as taught by you is unattainable.   6:33

O Krishna, since the mind is restless, turbulent, strong, and obstinate, it is as hard to regulate as the wind.   6:34

◆ *Krishna said:*

Indeed, the mind is restless and difficult to control, yet it can be disciplined through practice and nonattachment.   6:35

The yogic state is hard to achieve by a man who lacks mental control, and yet it can be reached with a disciplined mind that follows the proper method.   6:36

◆ *Arjuna asked:*

What happens to a person who is dedicated to yoga, but is unsuccessful in achieving its results because of restlessness and lack of control of the mind? 6:37

Confused in his pursuit of the inner self, is he not lost like a disappearing cloud? 6:38

O Krishna, please help me in resolving this doubt because there is no one else besides you who can completely destroy this confusion. 6:39

◆ *Krishna spoke:*

A man who is the doer of good deeds will not perish in this world or the next one. 6:40

He who is unsuccessful in the pursuit of yoga goes to the world of the meritorious and, after living there for a long time is reborn into a pure and prosperous family. 6:41

Or such a person might be born into a family of yogis who are endowed with wisdom. This kind of birth is hard to obtain in the world. 6:42

Here a person will recover wisdom acquired during former births and will strive once again to achieve the goals of yoga. 6:43

Because of this former wisdom, a man will be compelled to carry on with the yoga practice. Those who show inclination towards yoga are superior to the practitioners of the Vedic ritual.[23] 6:44

A yogi who perseveres in his effort, is purified of moral blemish. Being perfected by many births, he will reach the ultimate goal of life. 6:45

O Arjuna, since a yogi is superior to the ascetic, the learned, or the performer of rituals, be a yogi. 6:46

I regard a man to be the best of yogis whose heart is intent upon me and who devotedly sings my praises while seeking me. 6:47

---

[23]The four *Vedas* are the religious–philosophical books of the Hindus. They describe various rituals through which one could relate to the deity of one's choice.

Chapter VII

The Divine's Higher and Lower Natures

Summary:

One can obtain complete knowledge of the divine self through devotion and the practice of yoga. Krishna imparts this highest wisdom to Arjuna by drawing a distinction between the lower and the higher natures. Krishna's lower nature (*Prakriti*) is a combination of earth, water, fire, air, ether, mind, intellect, and ego; whereas the higher nature (divine self) is the support of all existence. The entire universe is strung on the divine self as flowers on a garland. The higher nature is the essence of touch, taste, smell, sight, and sound. It is the humanness in human beings, the wisdom in the wise, and the original seed in all beings. Under the spell of their lower natures, living beings are confused and, therefore, do not recognize their higher nature. When guided by their lower nature, they worship different deities. Krishna tells Arjuna that the worshippers of deities will go to them in due course of time, whereas those who are devoted to Krishna and know that he is omnipresent will gain mental harmony and true wisdom in this life.

Text:

◆ *Krishna spoke to Arjuna:*

Listen as to how you, by the practice of yoga and through absorption in me, can obtain certain and complete knowledge of me.   7:1

Once you acquire this wisdom from me, you won't need any other knowledge.   7:2

Out of thousands of people some make an effort to obtain this wisdom, but out of these, only a few are successful in knowing me.   7:3

My material nature[24] is constructed from the eight ingredients of earth, water, fire, air, ether, mind, intellect, and ego.   7:4

---

[24]Material nature (*Prakriti*) is synonymous with the "lower nature," "empirical self," and "bodily self." It consists of the three qualities of good (*sattva*), passion (*rajasa*) and dullness (*tamasa*).

26

This is my lower nature, in contrast to the divine nature, which supports the entire existing universe.   7:5

All creatures are born from the lower nature. Know therefore that I am both the creator and destroyer of everything in the universe.   7:6

There is nothing higher than me in all existence. All creatures of the universe are strung on me like pearls on a necklace.   7:7

I am the essence of water, the light in the sun and the moon, the syllable *Om*[25] in the scriptures,[26] the sound in the firmament and the humanness in the human being.   7:8

I am the fragrance in the earth and the brightness in the sun.
I am the life force in all creatures and the austerity in all ascetics.   7:9

I am the original seed in all creatures.
I am the wisdom in the wise and the splendor in the splendid.   7:10

I am the passionless might in the mighty and the righteous passion in all human beings.   7:11

Though the good (*sattvic*),[27] passionate (*rajasic*),[28] and inertial (*tamasic*)[29] states of nature are born of me, I am not in them, yet they are still in me.   7:12

Since the entire world is under the spell of these qualities of nature, human beings do not recognize my presence. I am beyond them.   7:13

This cosmic magic (*maya*)[30] of mine is difficult to penetrate, yet those who take shelter in me are able to break through this barrier.   7:14

Those who are evildoers, ignorant, or engulfed in the cosmic illusion do not surrender to me because they are guided by their own base nature.   7:15

There are four kinds of virtuous people who worship me: those in distress, those who seek knowledge, those who want wealth, and those who desire wisdom.   7:16

Of these, the seeker of wisdom, who is totally devoted to me, is preeminent because I am fond of the wise and the wisdom seeker is fond of me.   7:17

---

[25] *Om* is a mystical sound that is recited at the beginning and/or the end of a prayer.

[26] "Scriptures" refers to the *Vedas*, the earliest books of the Hindus.

[27] *Sattva* is one of the three components of material reality. Its predominance in a person predisposes him toward good deeds, reflection, and meditation.

[28] *Rajasa* is one of the three components of material reality. Its predominance in a person predisposes him toward restless activity.

[29] *Tamasa* is one of the three components of material reality. Its predominance in a person predisposes him toward dullness or laziness.

[30] *Maya* can be translated as "cosmic illusion" or "cosmic magic."

Though all four of them are noble, I prefer the person of wisdom because he is verily myself and furthermore he is totally engrossed in me and makes me the highest goal.   7:18

After many births and deaths, the person of wisdom comes to dwell in me, knowing that I am in all creatures. Such a person is a rarity among human beings.   7:19

Other people are restricted by their natures and are confused by desire. They enslave themselves to gods through the performance of various rituals.   7:20

O Arjuna, whosoever devotedly worships any god, I help strengthen his faith.   7:21

Propelled by this devotion, he who worships a particular deity and gets a reward, receives this reward from me.   7:22

Men of meager learning enjoy rewards temporarily. Men who offer worship to the gods, go to them; whereas my worshipers come to me.   7:23

Though I am unmanifest, the ignorant men believe that I possess a manifest form. They are unaware of my higher immutable nature.   7:24

Because I hide myself through cosmic magic, I am unmanifest to most people. The deluded ones do not recognize my immutable and imperishable being.   7:25

O Arjuna, I have knowledge of all beings of the past, the present, and the future; but no one knows me.   7:26

Engulfed in dichotomies of pain and pleasure or desire and passion, all creatures are born into this delusion.   7:27

All those virtuous people who have eliminated their evil deeds and have transcended these pairs of opposites worship me with complete devotion.   7:28

Those who seek freedom from the cycle of age and death take repose in me and thus obtain knowledge of the divine self and its activities.   7:29

Those who know that I am present in the physical, celestial, and ritualistic worlds are able to gain mental harmony and true knowledge of me at the time of their death.   7:30

Chapter VIII

Path to the Supreme Self

Summary:

At the beginning of this chapter, Arjuna raises seven major questions about the supreme self, which are answered by Krishna as follows: The supreme self is the immutable reality; the individual self is the divine spark at the core of one's being; the creative divine act produces all beings; the created world is perishable; consciousness is the essence of the deities; the source of all action in the body is Krishna; and one's focusing on Krishna at the time of death is the way to reach the supreme self. Moreover, Krishna tells Arjuna that through controlling the body, the vital breath, and the heart, and through unwavering contemplation, one can be absorbed into the supreme self. Therefore, when one devotes oneself completely to the supreme self, believes it to be all pervasive, and regards it as the highest goal of one's life, one will ultimately dwell in the supreme.

Text:

◆ *Arjuna asked Krishna:*

O highest of persons, please explain to me the nature of the supreme self,[31] the individual self,[32] the creative force,[33] the elements which constitute all beings,[34] and the divine.[35]   8:1

---

[31]This ultimate reality (*Brahman*) is synonymous with the expressions "the absolute being" and "the supreme self."

[32]An aspect of the supreme self residing at the core of one's being is called *adhyatma* or "the individual self."

[33]The word *karma* is translated as "the creative force." In the present context, *karma* means the "universal creative force" through which all beings are born.

[34]*Adhibhutas* are the five elements (earth, water, fire, air and ether) that constitute material reality.

[35]*Adhidaiva* means "the supreme being" that resides within a person. In this context, it is the consciousness of the supreme self that illuminates everything.

Will you also tell me the relationship of sacrifice to the body and the way the disciplined ones grasp your nature at the time of their death?   8:2

◆ *Krishna answered:*

The supreme self is the ultimate immutable reality, the individual self is this divine self within, and the creative force is the divine power that produces all creatures.   8:3

Perishability is the nature of the created world; consciousness is the nature of the divine, and I am the nature of sacrifice in the body.   8:4

If a man focuses on me at the time of death, he is sure to be assimilated into my being.   8:5

O Arjuna, whatever a man is engrossed in at the time of death, he will become that in his next life.   8:6

Therefore, keep your mind on me at all times and fight. When your heart and spirit are focused on me, you will certainly come to me in the end.   8:7

With a focused and unwavering mind, he who contemplates the supreme self will go toward it.   8:8

The supreme self is the ancient seer; it is smaller than the smallest; it is the creator of all; it's form is beyond comprehension and it possesses the color of the sun.   8:9

At the time of death, he who contemplates this supreme self with a disciplined mind, with concentrated devotion and with the life force centered between the eyebrows, reaches the supreme being.   8:10

I will describe to you the nature of the supreme self, which the teachers of the *Vedas* call the imperishable. Desirous of this state, the ascetics free themselves of passion by undergoing self-control.   8:11

A man who closes out the gates of the body, reposes the mind in the heart, centers the life force in the forehead, steadies himself through concentration, and utters the syllable *Om* while meditating on me departs from this world and enters my abode.   8:12,13

A yogi who is constantly preoccupied with me and has me as the focus of attention at all times reaches me easily.   8:14

Those who have achieved this stage of supreme perfection do not return to the impermanent world of sorrow.   8:15

All the created worlds go through the cycles of births and deaths, but a man who reaches me is never reborn.   8:16

The day and night of the creator are thousands of eons long. Those who grasp this truly understand days and nights.   8:17

When the day of the creator starts, the unmanifest gives birth to the manifest. When the night of the creator begins, the manifested dissolves into the unmanifest. 8:18

Different forms of existence are repeatedly born during the days and helplessly dissolve into nonexistence during the nights. 8:19

Another unmanifest lies beyond this unmanifest. The former is eternal while the latter is destructible. 8:20

This is called the imperishable supreme self, which is the highest goal of life. A man who achieves it never comes back. This is where I reside. 8:21

This supreme self, which is all pervasive, resides at the core of man's being and can be attained exclusively through devotion. 8:22

O Arjuna, I will describe to you the different paths followed by the departing yogis, who return and those who do not return. 8:23

A yogi who departs during the fire, the light, the day, the moonlit fortnight, or the six months of the northern sun, while possessing a knowledge of the supreme self, will reach the abode of the supreme being. 8:24

A yogi who departs during smoke, night, the dark half of the lunar fortnight, or the six months of the southern sun reaches the light of the moon and then returns. 8:25

The paths of darkness and light are eternally there. By one, a man returns, whereas by the other, he never returns. 8:26

He who has knowledge of these paths is not confused. Therefore, Arjuna, be focused through yoga. 8:27

The yogi who transcends the benefits accrued from the study of the *Vedas*, ritual, austerity, and charity reaches the supreme self. 8:28

Chapter IX

Wisdom and Worship

Summary:

Krishna reveals to Arjuna the profound religious wisdom, which is simple, immediately known, and everlasting. As the supreme being, Krishna has a dual nature. He is both unmanifest and all pervasive in the manifest universe. Though Krishna is the support of all creatures, he does not dwell in them. He creates the universe, supports it as long as it lasts, and destroys it at the end. Krishna performs these acts of creation and destruction repeatedly through his cosmic power. A sage who realizes the workings of Krishna's divine power in the universe, sings his praises and devotedly seeks him. Different people worship Krishna in their own unique ways. Those who offer worship to lesser deities go to them, and those who worship Krishna come to him after their death. Worship is of utmost importance. Any form of devotion shown to Krishna is amply rewarded. Even an evildoer can be elevated to the status of a sage if he offers devotion to Krishna. Therefore, Krishna tells Arjuna that if he sets his heart on him, becomes his devotee, and makes him the highest goal, he will ultimately be absorbed in him.

Text:

◆ *Krishna spoke to Arjuna:*

Since you are without hatred, I will reveal to you the secret of profound wisdom, knowing this, no harm will ever come to you.   9:1

This elevated wisdom is an ultimate mystery and is supremely sacred. It can be found through direct intuition, is in accord with tradition, is easy to follow, and is durable.   9:2

Those who show no faith in this doctrine fail to find me and get trapped into the birth and death cycle.   9:3

Though I am unmanifest, I pervade the manifest universe. All creatures exist in me. However, I do not exist in them.   9:4

Arjuna, try to grasp my divine mystery. Though all creatures are sustained by my spirit, they really do not dwell in me and I do not dwell in them.   9:5

Just as the great wind is spread all over the earth and yet is confined in one place, so are all creatures confined in me.   9:6

All creatures are dissolved into my nature at the end of the time cycle[36] and are given birth by me at the beginning of a new time cycle.   9:7

I repeatedly create a multitude of creatures through the power of my own nature.   9:8

These actions do not bind me, because I remain totally aloof and detached from them.   9:9

Under my guidance, all animate and inanimate beings are produced. In this way the world stays on its course.   9:10

The foolish misjudge my power when they see me in my human form, not realizing my divine aspect, which is the governor of all creatures.   9:11

Involved in worthless hopes, fruitless deeds, mindless knowledge, and thoughtless judgment, they are guided by their demonic natures.   9:12

The sages who are established in their divine nature regard me as the source of all creatures and offer me their constant devotion.   9:13

Some glorify me, sing my praises, devotedly bow before me, worship me, and resolutely seek me.   9:14

Some worship me as having a single form, while others worship me as possessing many forms. Each worships me in his or her own unique way.
                                                                        9:15

I am the ritual, the sacrifice, the holy food, the curative herb, the sacred hymn,[37] the clarified butter, the fire, and the offering.   9:16

---

[36]In Hindu mythology, the age of the universe between its birth and death is measured with a unit called a *yuga*. There are four different types of *yugas*. When the universe is created, it goes through *sat yuga*, the age of truth, which lasts for 1,728,000 years. It is followed by the *treta yuga*, where truth is a dominant feature. This *yuga* lasts for 1,296,000 years. This in turn is followed by the *dvapara yuga*, where truth and evil weigh equally. This *yuga* lasts for 864,000 years. The fourth *yuga* is called *kali yuga*, where evil predominates. It is the shortest time period and lasts for 432,000 years. All of them together constitute a *maha yuga*. One thousand *maha yugas* equal one time cycle, which is referred to as the day or night of the supreme self.

[37]*Mantra* (hymn) is a word or phrase that is an aid in meditation (e.g. *Om, Soham*).

I am the father, mother, sustainer, and grandparent of the universe. I am the wisdom sought by people. I am the sound *Om*,[38] the *Rig Veda*,[39] the *Sama Veda*,[40] and the *Yajur Veda*.[41]   9:17

I am also the goal, the sustainer, the governor, the seer, the companion, the beginning, the end, the resting abode, and the immutable seed.   9:18

I am the giver of heat. I stop and start the rain. I am nectar as well as death. I am both being and nonbeing.   9:19

The knowers of the three *Vedas* who had drunk the intoxicating juice,[42] having cleansed themselves of nonrighteousness, worship me in order to secure a place in heaven. They reach Indira's[43] house, where they enjoy the divine pleasures reserved only for gods.   9:20

After enjoying the expansive heavenly abode, the effect of their good deeds is depleted, whereupon they return to the mortal world again and get trapped into the birth–death cycle.   9:21

I give those who devotedly worship me and are solely absorbed in me what they need and enhance what they own.   9:22

All those who worship other deities are in fact worshiping me though they are using inappropriate means.   9:23

Since these people do not recognize me as the enjoyer of all sacrifice, they are therefore reborn.   9:24

Those who worship deities go to the deities; those who worship ancestors go to the ancestors; those who worship the spirits go to the spirits; and those who worship me come to me.   9:25

He who devotedly and lovingly brings me a leaf, a flower, a fruit, or even some water—I'll accept this offering happily.   9:26

Do your work, perform your sacrifice, indulge in charity, and offer your penance for my sake.   9:27

Freed from the bondage of action and disciplined in the path of renunciation, you will come to me.   9:28

[38] *Om* is a mystical sound that is chanted at the beginning and/or at end of a prayer. It is also considered to be the highest of mantras.

[39] The *Rig Veda* is the most philosophical of the four *Vedas*.

[40] The *Sama Veda* offers rules for singing the hymns.

[41] The *Yajur Veda* offers rules for performing the rituals and sacrifices.

[42] *Soma* is an intoxicating drink prepared from mushrooms. It was believed to have the power to give the user mystical vision or youthful vigor. It was first mentioned in the time of the *Vedas*.

[43] Indira is regarded as the king of gods. He is also a god of the thunderstorm.

All human beings are equal to me. I hate no one and love no one. Those who worship me with complete devotion abide in me and I abide in them.   9:29

Even when a doer of bad deeds worships me with full devotion, I regard this man to be a saint because he has taken the correct path.   9:30

He quickly becomes a virtuous person and achieves unlimited peace. O Arjuna, I declare this to be a fact: that he who is my devotee will not perish.   9:31

Even women, traders, and servants of lowly birth attain the highest goal if they take shelter in me.   9:32

How easy it is then for the holy scholars and devoted sages to attain this goal. Having been born into this perishable and painful world, you should devote yourself completely to me.   9:33

By setting your heart on me, becoming my devotee, adoring me, paying homage to me, and by making me your highest goal, you will ultimately be absorbed in me.   9:34

Chapter X

Glorious Manifestations of the Divine

Summary:

Krishna wants to offer Arjuna supreme words of wisdom regarding his manifestations. Though Krishna as the Lord is originless, everything has its being in him. He is the source of the seven sages and the four founders of the human race. Since Krishna is ubiquitous, he narrates to Arjuna the most significant of his manifestations: He is the divine spark at the core of each being; he is God Vishnu, the preserver; he is God Shiva, the destroyer; he is the *Sama Veda* of the *Vedas;* he is Bhrigu among the sages; he is the fig tree among the trees; he is king among human beings; and, he is Arjuna among the present assembled warriors. Since Krishna's divine manifestations are endless, Arjuna should be satisfied with knowing that the manifest universe represents only a tiny part of Krishna—the supreme being.

Text:

◆ *Krishna spoke:*

O mighty warrior Arjuna, listen to my words of wisdom. Since you are dear to me, I will tell you this for your benefit.　　　　　10:1

Neither the gods nor the great sages know my origin. Yet I am the original source of all of them.　　　　　10:2

Those who know me as the governor of the universe without origin or beginning are not puzzled and become free of all moral blemish.　10:3

I am the source of insight, knowledge, mental clarity, forgiveness, truth, self-control, equanimity, happiness, sorrow, renewal, death, fear, courage, health, even-mindedness, equilibrium, mortification, charity, and fame.　　　　　10:4,5

Out of the power of my mind, I created the seven ancient sages[44] and the four founders of the human race.[45] All other creatures came out of these.   10:6

A man with a focused mind clearly grasps my omnipresence and creative power.   10:7

The wise, who know that I am the causal source of everything and that everything springs forth from me, meditate on me.   10:8

Thinking of me constantly, devoting themselves completely, speaking of me repeatedly, and actively facilitating each other's enlightenment, they shall find contentment and happiness.   10:9

To those who are absorbed in me and lovingly want to sing my praises, I offer the yoga of discernment through which they can reach me. 10:10

Because I care about them, I reside in their hearts. Through this dwelling, I help burn their ignorance through the fire of wisdom. 10:11

◆ *Arjuna inquired:*

You are the supreme reality, the highest abode, the greatest purifier, the divine self, and the original God.   10:12

This fact is narrated by the epic poet Vyasa, all the sages,[46] and you. 10:13

I believe everything that you have told me. O Blessed One, neither the gods nor the demons grasp your true nature.   10:14

O Krishna, since you are the source of all creatures, the nurturer of all beings, the god of gods, the highest divine self, you alone have knowledge of yourself.   10:15

Please help me see your divine manifestations through which you display your omnipresence in the universe.   10:16

O Blessed One, tell me how I should worship you so as to know your essence. Which aspects of you should I meditate upon?   10:17

Could you help me to understand your mystical powers and manifestations? I want to listen closely to your edifying words.   10:18

---

[44]In Hindu mythology, the seven ancient sages were born from the consciousness of the supreme self. After they were created, the rest of creation originated from them.

[45]These four ancient Manus are responsible for creating all human beings.

[46]Narada, Asita, Devala, and Vyasa are the great seers in Hindu mythology, who have narrated the wisdom concerning the nature of the supreme self and its manifestations.

◆ *Krishna answered:*

Since my ubiquity is limitless, I will narrate to you only the most important manifestations of me.   10:19

O Arjuna, I am the divine self residing at the core of each being. I am the beginning, the middle, and the end of all creation.   10:20

I am Vishnu among the great deities; I am the sun among celestial bodies; I am the king of gods of storm; and I am the moon among the shining heavenly bodies.   10:21

I am the *Sama Veda* among the *Vedas;* I am Indira among the gods; I am the mind among the senses; and I am consciousness among the living. 10:22

I am Shiva among the gods of construction and destruction; I am the king among the gods of wealth; I am the fire among the eight light-giving gods; and I am Mt. Meru among the mountains.   10:23

I am Brihaspati among the priests; I am Skanda among the war commanders; and I am the ocean among lakes.   10:24

I am Bhrigu among the great sages; I am the single syllable *Om* among all languages; I am the silent prayer among the rituals; and I am the Himalayas among the steadfast.   10:25

I am the fig tree within a forest; I am Narada among the divine sages; I am Chitraratha among heavenly musicians; and I am Kapila among the seers.   10:26

I am the immortal stallion (born of elixir) among the horses; I am Airawata among elephants; and I am a king among commoners.   10:27

I am a thunderbolt among weapons; I am a cow of plenty among cows; I am the god of love among life-givers; and I am Vasuki among snakes.   10:28

I am Ananta among serpents; I am Varuna among water-deities; I am Aryaman among the dead ancestors; and I am Yama among the controllers of life and death.   10:29

I am Prahlada among the demons; I am time among reckoners; I am lion among beasts; and I am eagle among birds.   10:30

I am the wind among the purifiers; I am the weapon-bearing Rama among warriors; I am the crocodile among fish; and I am the Ganges among the rivers.   10:31

O Arjuna, I am the beginning, the middle, and the end of all creatures; I am the wisdom of the divine self among all knowledge; and I am the truth among debaters.   10:32

I am the letter A in the alphabet; I am the coupling of compounds; I am the eternal time and the omniscient god who can see in all four directions.   10:33

I am the all-encroaching death; I am the source of all future births; and I am the female's virtues such as fame, fortune, speech, reminiscence, intelligence, steadfastness, and patience.   10:34

I am the ritural chant among the hymns; I am Gayatri among meters; I am the sacred month among months; and I am the spring among seasons.   10:35

I am the gambling spirit among the cheaters; I am the splendor among the splendid; I am the victory, the courage, and the goodness in the virtuous.   10:36

I am Krishna among the Yadavas; I am Arjuna among the Pandavas; I am Vyasa among the seers; and I am Shuka among the poets.   10:37

I am the staff held in the hand of the controller; I am the good sense in those who desire victory; I am the silence of the mysterious; and I am the knowledge of the wise.   10:38

O Arjuna, I am the seed in all beings. Everything animate or inanimate exists because of me.   10:39

My divine manifestations are unlimited. I have given you only a sampling of my divine glory.   10:40

Whosoever possesses magnificence, grace, and vigor has obtained it from a fraction of my splendor.   10:41

O Arjuna, what need is there for you to know more about me? You should be satisfied with the knowledge that I create this entire universe through a tiny part of me.   10:42

Chapter XI

Intuitive Vision of the Cosmic Form

Summary:

Arjuna wishes to have a vision of Krishna's cosmic form. Since this form cannot be seen with ordinary eyes, Krishna gives Arjuna a third eye or divine sight. Arjuna is then able to see this cosmic form as multicolored and possessing many shapes, mouths, and eyes. While bedecked with beautiful ornaments and divine weapons, it displays many wondrous feats. Many different creatures, deities, and universes dwell in it. This infinite form is without a beginning, middle, or end; even if a thousand suns lit up the sky at the same time, it would not be equal to the splendor of this cosmic form. Arjuna reacts to this revelation in two different ways. On one hand, he is thoroughly convinced that Krishna is the ultimate reality, the goal of our seeking, and the final resting place for all beings. On the other hand, he is terrified by the burning mouths and flaming tongues of this form and requests Krishna to display his gentler human form. Krishna tells Arjuna that this cosmic form cannot be seen through the knowledge of the *Vedas,* the performance of rituals, or the giving of gifts. However, it is easily available to anyone who approaches Krishna with full devotion by acting for him, holding him to be the ultimate goal, showering love on him, and taking repose in him.

Text:

◆ *Arjuna spoke to Krishna:*

You have removed all of my confusion by compassionately and gracefully conveying to me the secret knowledge of the supreme self.   11:1

O Krishna, I have heard you talk about the creation and dissolution of all creatures as well as about your inexhaustible greatness.   11:2

I want to see your cosmic form, which you had described to me earlier.   11:3

If I am worthy of this vision, would you please reveal it to me?   11:4

◆ *Krishna answered:*

Look at my manifold forms, which are multicolored and have multifarious shapes. 11:5

See the gods of sun, fire, light, thunder, storm, and the twin gods of dawn.[47]
See these and many other marvels that no one has seen before. 11:6

See the entire universe of moving and unmoving beings residing in me.
See whatever you are desirous of seeing. 11:7

Since you will be unable to see my cosmic form with your ordinary eyes,
I will give you divine sight for this revelation. 11:8

◆ *While speaking to Arjuna in this manner, Krishna revealed his cosmic form to him.* 11:9

It had many mouths and eyes and displayed many wondrous feats. It was bedecked with beautiful ornaments and divine weapons. 11:10

Adorned with celestial garlands, clothes, and perfumes, this cosmic form faced every direction at once. 11:11

Even if a thousand suns lit up the sky at the same time, it would not compare to the splendor of this cosmic form. 11:12

Arjuna saw many creatures of the universe dwelling in Krishna's body. 11:13

Overwhelmed with amazement and awe, shaken by the vision, with bowed head and folded hands, Arjuna said: 11:14

Residing in your body, I see all the gods, including the creator[48] sitting on the lotus flower. The seers and the divine serpents are there too. 11:15

I see your countless arms, bellies, mouths, and eyes. I see your infinite form without a beginning, middle, or end. I also see your all pervasive form in which the universe rests. 11:16

I see you adorned with a crown, a mace, and a discus. You are aglow with brilliant light that hurts my mortal eyes, and you are encircled with a burning fire like the sun. 11:17

[47]In Sanskrit, they are called *Ashvins*. In Hindu mythology, they are two celestial horsemen who usher in the dawn each morning.

[48]In Hindu mythology, Brahman (the supreme self), acts as the creator, preserver, and destroyer of the universe. In his function as a creator, he is called Brahma.

You are the ultimate reality, the goal that everyone should seek, the resting place for all creatures, the defender of eternal law, and the most supreme person.   11:18

You are without beginning, middle, or end; you are all powerful; the moon and sun are your eyes, and the entire universe is an offering to the flaming fire of your mouth.   11:19

You encompass the space between earth and sky from every direction. The three worlds[49] tremble when your marvelous and terrifying form is near.   11:20

A throng of deities dwells in you—those who are afraid pray to you with folded hands, while groups of sages and ascetics bestow praises on you.   11:21

The evil destroying deities, the celestial gods, the beneficent ones, the celestial beings, the twin gods of dawn, the gods of storm, the ancestors, the celestial musicians, the supernatural beings, and the demons are all in awe of your majestic appearance.   11:22

The sight of your enormous form consisting of many mouths, eyes, arms, thighs, stomachs, and feet makes the worlds shake, and so do I.   11:23

When I observe your multicolored being spread out in the firmament with a wide open mouth and terrifying eyes, my inner self quivers; concentration and tranquility escape me.   11:24

Seeing your mouths with blazing fangs that resemble the burning fires of destruction, I have lost both my direction and peace. Please have mercy on me, because you are the final resting place for all creatures.   11:25

Dhritarashtra's sons, along with kings and warriors such as Bhishma, Drona, Karna, and many of our great soldiers, are entering into your mouth, where they are crushed into powder by your great fangs. 11:26,27

Just as overflooded streams rush toward the ocean in a fury, so do these great warriors rush toward the burning fire in your mouth.   11:28

Just as moths speed toward a fire to be destroyed by it, all of these people rush toward your mouth unaware of their impending destruction. 11:29

Your burning mouths and flaming tongues are consuming all the worlds. The light of your fire is scorching everything and yet spreading its glow evenly over the universe.   11:30

Who are you in this terrifying form? I respectfully bow before you and ask you to have mercy on me. I do want to understand your original form, but I do not understand what I see.   11:31

---

[49]Reference is made to the earthly, atmospheric, and heavenly worlds.

◆ *Krishna replied:*

I am the time that destroys everything; I have arrived here to devour everything. Even if you do not fight with all these great warriors, they will cease to exist in due time. 11:32

Therefore, stand up and earn your fame. Destroy your enemies and take back your kingdom. All of these warriors have already been destroyed by me, so act as my vehicle to complete my work. 11:33

Arjuna, get ready. Fight such great warriors as Drona, Bhishma, Jayadratha, and Karna without hesitation because they are already killed by me. If you battle these men, then you are assured of victory. 11:34

◆ *Sanjaya[50] continued:*

Upon hearing these words, Arjuna, while still trembling with fright, bowed before Krishna and said: 11:35

"The entire universe is rejoicing in being able to sing your praises. The evildoers are fleeing in all directions and those who became perfect are offering their praises to you. 11:36

Why should not they praise and adore you? You are higher than the original creator of the universe.[51] You are the ultimate being, the god of gods, and the resting place for all creatures. You encompass all that is, all that is not, and all that is yet to be. 11:37

You are the first god, the supreme person, the final repose for all creatures. You are the seer, the seen—the ultimate goal of life itself. The entire universe is encompassed by your infinite form. 11:38

You are the progenitor of the gods of wind, death, fire, water, and moon. I offer my devotion to you a thousand times. 11:39

My devotion flows towards you from the back, the front, and all other sides. You are omnipotent and all pervasive. 11:40

Not realizing your ultimate majesty, I ignorantly and fondly called you Krishna, companion, or friend. 11:41

I might have been disrespectful to you while jesting, resting, eating, or walking whether alone or in the company of others, and for this, I ask your forgiveness. 11:42

---

[50]Sanjaya is the minister of the blind king Dhritarashtra who has been given divine sight by the sage Vyasa so that he could describe the entire battle to the blind king.

[51]In Hindu mythology, Brahma is the Creator of the Universe.

You are the origin of the animate and inanimate worlds. You are the greatest teacher fit for worship. No one is equal or better than you in all three worlds.   11:43

Therefore, I bow before you and ask you to forgive me. Be kind to me like a father to a son, a friend to a friend, or a lover to a beloved.   11:44

I rejoice at seeing your cosmic form, which no one has seen before, and yet I am terrified of it. Please be merciful and reveal your familiar human figure to me.   11:45

I want to see your four-armed form, where you are wearing the crown and your hands are holding the mace and the discus."   11:46

◆ *Krishna spoke:*

You have been privileged to see this cosmic form through my divine power. You are the only person who has seen me as luminous, all-encompassing, limitless, and primal.   11:47

In this world, a revelation of me is not possible through the *Vedas* or rituals, or academic studies, or gifts, or austerities.   11:48

Do not be afraid or confused by my awesome form. Get rid of your fear, and rejoice at seeing my familiar human form.   11:49

◆ *Sanjaya spoke:*

Krishna showed his human form to Arjuna, which consoled him.   11:50

◆ *Arjuna said:*

By seeing your gentle human form, I have come back to my senses, and my heart is at peace.   11:51

◆ *Krishna replied:*

It is impossible for anyone to see this cosmic form that you have just seen. Even the gods long to have this kind of revelation.   11:52

This great vision of me that you have just had is not possible through the *Vedas,* rituals, or common gifts.   11:53

But those who approach me with full devotion can easily have a revelation of my cosmic form.   11:54

Anyone who acts for me, holds me as his ultimate goal, showers love on me, and is free from attraction or repulsion will ultimately take repose in me.   11:55

Chapter XII

Path of Devotion

Summary:

Arjuna wants to know from Krishna whether a devotee should worship his personal or unmanifest absolute form. Krishna tells Arjuna that since human beings are mortal, it is more difficult for them to worship the unmanifest form than the personal form. As Krishna prefers personal devotion, he discusses this kind of worship by distinguishing between ideal and ordinary devotees. Ideal devotees are those who worship him with complete devotion, perform their actions for his sake, regard him as their supreme end, and are totally engrossed in him. The conditions for the ordinary devotees are simpler. Hence, they can reach Krishna in one of the following ways: By focusing their hearts and minds on him; by performing an action with the intent of serving him; by renouncing an action's rewards; by hating no one and showing friendship toward all; by transcending sensual craving, anger, fear, hate, grief, and desire, by regarding friend or foe, honor or dishonor, happiness or suffering alike; by being balanced in praise or blame, and by being content, serene, and resolute. Krishna tells Arjuna that all those devotees who regard him as their final goal and faithfully follow the aforementioned wisdom are closest to his heart.

Text:

◆ *Arjuna asked:*

Some worship your personal form with complete devotion, whereas others worship your unmanifest absolute form. Please tell me which one of these two is superior.   12:1

◆ *Krishna replied:*

Those whose minds are constantly and faithfully involved in showering love on me are perfect worshippers.   12:2

Others reach me by worshipping my indestructible, undefinable, unmanifest, all-pervasive, indescribable, immutable, and eternal absolute form.   12:3

They reach me too by disciplining their senses, adopting an amiable attitude toward others, and by engaging themselves in the service of others.   12:4

The path of those who seek the unmanifest absolute is much more difficult because it is hard for mortal beings to grasp the infinite.   12:5

Those who perform their actions for me, worship me with total devotion, regard me as their supreme end, and are totally engrossed in me are delivered by me from the birth–death cycle.   12:6,7

If your heart and mind are constantly focused on me, you are sure to rest within me eternally.   12:8

If you find it difficult to keep your mind steadily focused on me, then learn this concentration through yoga.   12:9

If the art of concentration is cumbersome, then at least try to perform each action with the intent of serving me. This path also leads toward me.   12:10

If you are incapable of doing even this, then take repose in me. With a disciplined heart and mind, perform each action by renouncing its fruits.   12:11

Knowledge is better than concentration; meditation is better than knowledge; and renunciation of the fruits of action is better than meditation.   12:12

He who hates no one, is friendly toward all, is detached from possessions and egoism, is balanced in pleasure and pain, is content, serene, and resolute, and whose heart and mind are completely devoted to me is closest to me.   12:13,14

He who is not afraid of people, who has transcended sensual craving, anger, fear, and distress, is also dear to me.   12:15

He who is content, pure, skillful, detached, and steadfast, and devotedly performs actions without seeking a reward is very near to my heart.   12:16

He who is beyond love or hate, grief or desire, is detached from good or evil, and is devoted to me is also dear to me.   12:17

He who regards friend or foe, honor or dishonor, heat or cold, happiness or suffering alike is also favored by me.   12:18

He who is balanced in praise or blame, is silent, is content with his life, has no fixed home, and is devoted to me, is cherished by me.   12:19

All those devotees who regard me as their final goal and follow this wisdom faithfully are highly esteemed by me.   12:20

Chapter XIII

The Body and Its Controller

Summary:

Arjuna wants to learn from Krishna the nature of the body, the controller of the body, materiality, consciousness, knowledge, and the objects of knowledge. He is told that the body is made up of the intellect, the ego, the mind, the five sense organs, the five motor organs, the five essences of action, and the five gross material elements. More specifically, materiality and consciousness are the two separate and eternal realities that together make up a human being. Materiality produces all objects, creatures, and human bodies. In contrast, consciousness, which lacks all material constitutive elements, is the experiencer of both pleasure and pain. Consciousness experiences the universe through the body, which serves as a vehicle. As it resides in the body, it is called the witness or the experiencer. It is this consciousness within each body that, like the sun, illuminates all the elements of the body. Krishna then informs Arjuna that this consciousness, which is the imperishable divine self, is the real controller of the body. Though it resides inside the body, it is untouched by physical action. One who understands this relationship between the body and its controller and between materiality and consciousness truly grasps the nature of the supreme self.

Text:

◆ *Arjuna asked Krishna:*

Kindly describe to me the nature of materiality,[52] consciousness,[53] the human body,[54] the controller of the body,[55] knowledge,[56] and the object of knowledge.[57]   13:1

---

[52]The word *prakriti* is translated as the "material reality" of the universe. *Prakriti* consists of three components of good (*sattva*), passion (*rajasa*), and dullness (*tamasa*). Through various combinations of these components, different objects and creatures are formed in the world.

[53]The word *purusha* is translated as the "consciousness" that experiences the universe. *Purusha* is the "divine spark" in each individual person.

(continued)

◆ *Krishna replied:*

The human body is the field, and one who masters it is its controller.   13:2

Arjuna, you should know that I am the controller of the body in each person. All those who grasp this distinction between the body and its controller possess true wisdom.   13:3

Now I will describe to you the nature of the human body, its constitutive elements, their origin, the nature of the controller, and its powers. 13:4

The sages of the *Vedas* have extolled them through various hymns, and other scriptures have offered definitive descriptions in support of them too.   13:5

The constitutive elements of the body are intellect, ego, mind,[58] the five sense organs (eye, ear, nose, tongue, and skin), the five motor organs (hand, foot, mouth, anus, and genital organ), the five gross elements (earth, water, fire, air, and ether), the five essences of action (sound, touch, color, taste, and smell), and the conglomeration of desire, repulsion, pleasure, pain, physicality, and consciousness.   13:6,7

Self-effacement, honesty, harmlessness, patience, simplicity, devotion to one's teacher, purity, complete control of the mind and senses;   13:8

Absence of lust and egoism, an awareness of the shortcomings of birth, death, old age, and disease;   13:9

Total detachment from children, spouse, and home; maintenance of complete equilibrium while facing either disturbing or pleasant events; 13:10

Complete devotion to me, spending time in places of pilgrimage, staying away from crowds;   13:11

Always seeking the knowledge of the supreme self, and regarding it to be the only truth, all this is called knowledge and the opposite is ignorance.   13:12

---

[54]The word *kshetra* is translated as the "field or vehicle" through which consciousness operates in the world. *Kshetra* also means the "human body" in contrast to consciousness.

[55]The word *kshetrajna* is translated as "one who controls" or knows the *kshetra* or "field." It is consciousness (*purusha*) in each body, which is its controller or knower.

[56]The word *jnanam* means "knowledge," which can be further subdivided into false knowledge or true knowledge.

[57]The word *jneyam* means "object of knowledge" or "that which is to be known."

[58]Our body performs both psychological and physical functions. The psychological part of the body works through the faculties of *buddhi* (intellect), *ahamkara* (ego), and *manas* (mind). When information is collected by the sense or motor organs, it is deposited in the *manas* (mind) part, which categorizes this knowledge. Through the sense of possession, the *ahamkara* (ego) part makes this knowledge its own and stores it in the *buddhi* (intellect) part.

Now I will describe to you the object of knowledge through which you will obtain salvation. It is the supreme self—which is neither being nor nonbeing.   13:13

Because it is all pervasive, the universe is covered by its hands, feet, eyes, ears, faces and heads.   13:14

Though it has none of the senses, it has the qualities of the senses; it is totally detached, yet it supports everything; it is devoid of the constitutive material elements, yet it experiences them.   13:15

It resides inside and outside every creature. It moves without moving. It is extremely subtle and cannot be grasped. It is very far and yet very close.   13:16

It is one and many. It is the creator, preserver, and destroyer of all beings.   13:17

It is beyond all darkness and is the source of all light. It is knowledge, the object of knowledge, and the goal of knowledge. It lies at the core of one's being.   13:18

I have given you a brief description of the field, the knowledge of it, and the object of knowledge. Devotees who are able to grasp this knowledge find repose in my nature.   13:19

The materiality and consciousness have no beginning. All objects and creatures are born out of materiality.   13:20

Materiality is the producer of the constitutive material elements, whereas consciousness is the experiencer of pleasure and pain.   13:21

As consciousness resides in the material self, it experiences the universe through this body. Its attachment to the material self is responsible for future higher or lower births.[59]   13:22

The consciousness residing in the material body is called the witness, consenter, sustainer, experiencer, supreme god, and highest person.   13:23

He who grasps the nature of consciousness, the material self and its constitutive elements, though involved in ordinary activities, is able to extricate himself from the birth–death cycle.   13:24

Some reach the divine self by following the path of devotion, whereas others follow the path of knowledge, and still others follow the path of action.   13:25

Furthermore, others who are unaware of these paths, but have heard of this doctrine and follow it faithfully, will also reach their salvation. 13:26

---

[59]A Hindu believes that a person is born into a higher or lower caste depending upon the actions or deeds performed in a previous life.

O Arjuna, all mobile and immobile creatures are born out of the union of the body (field) and the controller of the body (field).[60]   13:27

He who grasps the fact that the supreme self, which is present in everything, does not perish when everything else perishes, truly understands.   13:28

He who sees the supreme self to be resting equally in all creatures, does not go astray in achieving the highest goal of life.   13:29

He who aptly discerns that it is the materiality which performs all actions and that the conscious self does not do anything, truly understands.   13:30

When a man is able to see the one residing in the many and the many as the extension of the one, then such a person is in touch with the divine self.   13:31

The divine self, which is without beginning and without the material elements, is imperishable. Though it resides in the body, it is untouched by the body's actions.   13:32

Just as ever-present space is unaffected by the objects it touches, so is the divine self untouched by the material elements.   13:33

Just as the sun lights up the entire universe, so does the controller of the body illuminate all the elements of the body.   13:34

Those with a discerning eye who are able to see this difference between the body and its controller and between materiality and consciousness are sure to reach the abode of the supreme being.   13:35

[60]The word *kshetza* is translated as the "field" through which consciousness operates in the world.

Chapter XIV

The Three Components of the Material Reality

Summary:

Krishna wants to offer Arjuna a deep insight into the nature of the material reality and its component parts because such a knowledge is conducive to one's salvation. According to Krishna, all beings are born when he, as the father, plants a seed into the womb of the material reality. The three qualities of pure joy (*sattva*), restless activity (*rajasa*), and dullness (*tamasa*) constitute both this material reality and the human body. The divine self, or consciousness, expresses itself in the body through these three component parts. When the divine self illuminates pure joy, a person becomes attached to earthly happiness and knowledge; when the divine self illuminates restless activity, a person becomes attached to the world through action; and when the divine self illuminates dullness, a person becomes attached to the world through doubt and laziness. Joy, action, and dullness are the three components of materiality that bind us to the world. The predominance of any of these qualities in a person determines one's attitudes, actions, likes, and dislikes during one's lifetime. Even when a person dies, the fate waiting in the next world is determined by these qualities. However, Krishna says that a wise person is able to break the stronghold of these qualities by observing them in a detached way, by being balanced in pain or pleasure, praise or blame, honor or dishonor, by treating friend and foe alike, and by being unattached to worldly activities. By understanding and mastering these components of the material reality, a wise person is able to replace the suffering of birth, death, disease, and old age with the joy of immortal existence.

Text:

◆ *Krishna said:*

Now I will impart to you deep wisdom with which the great seers have reached supreme perfection. 14:1

Those who become part of me through this wisdom will not be reborn or die during the creation or dissolution of the universe. 14:2

The primal material reality is the womb. When I place my seed there, all creatures are born.   14:3

The multitude of life, which is produced in different wombs, is in actuality the great womb of the material reality, and I am the seed-giving father.   14:4

Joy,[61] restless activity,[62] and dullness[63] are the three ingredients that make up the material reality. They constitute the human body. Through them, the divine self gets attached to the body.   14:5

Joy, being pure, represents luminosity and health. It binds a man to earthly happiness and knowledge.   14:6

Restless activity, being passionate, produces agitative craving and attraction. It binds a man to the world through physical action.   14:7

Dullness, being ignorance, produces confusion. It binds a man to the universe through doubt, laziness, and sleep.   14:8

Goodness through joy, passion through action, and dullness through negligence bind a man to this world.   14:9

Goodness prevails when pure joy dominates restless activity and dullness. Passion prevails when restless activity dominates joy and dullness. Negligence prevails when dullness dominates joy and activity.   14:10

Joy is said to prevail in a man whose senses are illumined by the light of knowledge.   14:11

Activity is said to prevail in a man who is greedy, active, restless, and is constantly seeking.   14:12

Dullness is said to prevail in a man who lacks insight, initiative, attention, and clarity of mind.   14:13

When a man with the predominance of joy dies, he goes to the world where the wise reside.   14:14

When a man with the predominance of restless activity dies, he goes to the world where the people prone to activity reside. When a man with the predominance of dullness dies, he is reincarnated among the ignorant ones.   14:15

The reward of joyful action is pure bliss, of restless activity is pain, and of dullness is ignorance.   14:16

---

[61] *Sattva,* translated as "pure joy" or "goodness," is one of the three material components of all created beings. Its predominance predisposes one toward thinking, reflection, or meditation.

[62] *Rajasa,* translated as "restless activity" or "passion," is one of the three material components of all created beings. Its predominance predisposes a person toward agitative activity.

[63] *Tamasa,* translated as "dullness" or "inertia," is one of the three material components of reality. Its predominance predisposes a person toward dullness or laziness.

Pure joy produces knowledge, agitative activity gives rise to greed, and dullness causes bewilderment and confusion.   14:17

A joyful man moves up to the higher world, an active man remains in the middle world, and a dull man goes to the lower world.   14:18

A wise man who sees the three qualities of joy, activity, and dullness as the workhorses of the universe and who also sees what lies beyond these qualities will ultimately rest in me.   14:19

When the three qualities of joy, activity, and dullness are mastered by a wise man, the suffering of birth, death, and old age will be replaced by the delight of immortal existence.   14:20

◆ *Arjuna inquired:*

How is a man who has transcended these three qualities set apart from everyone else? How does such a man behave? In what ways are these qualities transcended?   14:21

◆ *Krishna replied:*

A man is said to have transcended the three qualities when he is not repelled by the arousal of joy, activity, or dullness in himself and does not crave them when they are gone.   14:22

This man, while being detached, observes the working of the three qualities in the universe and is still centered.   14:23

He maintains a balance in terms of pain or pleasure, has equipoise, values a piece of clay, gold, and stone equally, and is unperturbed by praise or blame.   14:24

He treats honor and dishonor alike, is equable toward friends and foes, and is unattached to all worldly activity.   14:25

A man who adores me with total devotion and performs all actions for me transcends the three qualities and is prepared to be absorbed into the supreme self.   14:26

For I am the home of the immortal and immutable supreme self; I am the home of eternal law and infinite bliss.   14:27

Chapter XV

The Cosmic Fig Tree

Summary:

Krishna tells Arjuna the story of a cosmic fig tree whose roots are in heaven while its branches are spread out into the earth. The three qualities of joy, activity, and dullness give it nourishment. Some of its roots, which stretch toward the earth, make human action possible. This tree symbolizes the ever-giving generous universe into which human beings are born. Through our desires, wishes, and sense of possession, we get attached to the universe. This entanglement results in misery and unhappiness. Though a large majority of people fail to grasp the mysterious nature of this tree, a wise man solves this puzzle with the sharp sword of detachment. Such a man knows how to take delight in everything without ever getting attached to anything. According to Krishna this detachment can be cultivated by freeing oneself from egoism and greed, by conquering attachment and passion, and by centering one's mind on the divine self. When its nature is properly grasped, the cosmic fig tree could become a path to the realization of the supreme self. Here Krishna develops the notion of three different kinds of selves. First, there is the empirical or bodily self, which is destructible; second, there is the divine spark residing within each person, which constitutes the imperishable self; and third, there is the supreme self, which is the master controller of the other two. One who lives in this universe by taking delight in everything while remaining aloof, and who knows the difference between the supreme self and the other two selves, has the correct knowledge to reach Krishna's peaceful abode.

Text:

◆ *Krishna spoke:*

O Arjuna, let me tell you the story about a cosmic fig tree whose roots are hidden in the heaven above, whose branches are spread toward the earth, and whose leaves are the Vedic hymns. He who grasps this—grasps the *Vedas*.   15:1

Its branches are extended toward the sky and the ground. The three qualities of joy, restless activity, and dullness give it nourishment, while some of its roots, which stretch below into the human world, make action possible. 15:2

The shape, origin, end, and foundation of this tree are beyond human comprehension. A wise man who cuts this tree with the sharp sword of detachment will find a place of repose in the universe. 15:3

Once such a refuge is found, he will never return to the mortal world because the primal spirit, which is the original source of all activity, becomes the dwelling place for the wise man. 15:4

A man who has freed himself of egoism and greed, conquered attachment and passion, centered his mind on the divine self, and transcended the dualities of attraction and repulsion, will reach my supreme resting place. 15:5

My supreme dwelling is not illuminated by the sun, moon, or fire. He who reaches my home will never want to return to the mortal world. 15:6

A spark of my divine self enters the physical world. It unites with a body through the five sense organs and the mind. 15:7

The divine self enters a physical body as its master. When it leaves a body, it takes with it the five senses and the mind like a breeze that carries with it a sweet scent of spring's blossoms. 15:8

The divine self experiences tangible objects through the nose, mouth, skin, eye, ear, and mind. 15:9

The divine self's constant transmigration from one body to another and its use of the physical body as a vehicle is hardly understood by the ignorant, whereas it is easily grasped by the wise. 15:10

Those with focused mind gain this understanding through effort, whereas ignorant ones cannot achieve it even through great struggle. 15:11

The light residing in sun, moon, and fire, through which the entire universe is illuminated, is my light. 15:12

By injecting my vital energy into the earth, I support all living creatures. And by becoming the intoxicating soma-juice,[64] I nourish all herbs and plant life. 15:13

I am the digestive fire in all living beings. I mingle with the movement of breath to digest different kinds of food. 15:14

I reside in the hearts of all living creatures. I am the creator and destroyer of both memory and knowledge. I am the highest knowledge

---

[64]*Soma* is an intoxicating drink prepared from mushrooms. It is first mentioned in the *Vedas*.

to be known through the *Vedas;* I am the author of the *Vedanta,* and the knower of the *Vedas.*   15:15

There are two kinds of selves in the world. The first kind is destructible, whereas the second one is indestructible. The physical body is the destructible self, whereas the divine spark within a person constitutes the indestructible self.   15:16

There is also the third kind of self, which is the supreme person. This self is the master controller that pervades and supports the three worlds.   15:17

Since I transcend both the destructible and the indestructible selves, I am called the supreme person.[65]   15:18

He who has transcended his ignorance and knows me as the supreme person has the correct knowledge. Such a man offers his heartfelt devotion to me.   15:19

O Arjuna, I have imparted to you this secret wisdom; knowing this, a man will be enlightened and will complete his highest task in this mortal world.   15:20

---

[65]The word used for the supreme person is *Purushottama.* Since Krishna transcends both the material self and the divine self and is also the controller of these two, he is regarded as *Purushottama*—the supreme person.

Chapter XVI

Sage-like and Unsage-like Endowments

Summary:

According to Krishna, two types of people are born into this world. Some are endowed with sage-like attributes, while others have unsage-like qualities. One who is sage-like possesses fearlessness, pure heartedness, self-restraint, simplicity, nonviolence, truthfulness, unpretentiousness, charitableness, and lack of pride. Such a person is assured of salvation. On the other hand, one who is unsage-like possesses deceptiveness, pride, hostility, aggressiveness, egoism, superficiality, vanity, ambitiousness, and selfish craving. Such a person is assured of bondage. Moreover, the unsage-like person believes that the universe is without a foundation or god; that moral values are arbitrary, and that the goal of life is the satisfaction of selfish desires. Guided by these wrong views, and being filled with pride, passion, and anger, these people spend their lives in the satisfaction of lustful cravings. Krishna tells Arjuna that he hurls these people repeatedly into the birth–death cycle. While living in this world, a person must not indulge in lustful passion, anger, and greed because these vices are responsible for a person's downfall. One who promises to eradicate these three unsage-like qualities in order to improve himself according to the rules of the holy books is certain to reach the highest goal of life. Therefore, Arjuna, by performing your preordained duties as dictated by the holy scriptures, you earn your salvation.

Text:

◆ *Krishna spoke:*

Those who are born with the sage-like nature possess the traits of fearlessness, pure heartedness, persistence in the pursuit of knowledge, benevolence, self-discipline, sacrifice, introspection, austerity, uprightness;   16:1

Harmlessness, truthfulness, non-combativeness, relinquishment, peacefulness, non-slanderousness, helpfulness toward living beings, abstinence from craving, kindness, unpretentiousness, dependability; 16:2

Vitality, forgiveness, boldness, purity, non-maliciousness, and minimal vanity.   16:3

Those who are born with the unsage-like nature possess the qualities of deceptiveness, pride, hostility, harsh speech, and ignorance.   16:4

Those endowed with sage-like qualities are assured of salvation, whereas the ones with unsage-like qualities are assured of bondage. O Arjuna, you need not be afraid, because you are born with sage-like qualities.   16:5

Two types of men are born into this world. They are classified as the sage-like and the unsage-like. I have enumerated to you the sage-like qualities; now I will describe to you the unsage-like qualities.   16:6

An unsage-like man is confused about initiating a good action or resisting a bad action. He does not take part in reflection, good conduct, or truth.   16:7

An unsage-like man believes that the universe is without any real substance, foundation, or god. To him, it is born out of lustful desire.   16:8

By embracing this false view, this lowly person, who is entrenched in ignorance and hostile action, desires to destroy the world.   16:9

When driven by this insatiable craving, embellished by superficiality, vanity, and ambitiousness, an unsage-like man pursues everything with impure motives.   16:10

Overburdened by afflictions, which can cease only at the time of death, an unsage-like man, who is driven by lustful desire, regards his gratification to be the highest goal in life.   16:11

An unsage-like man is ensnared by various cravings, which are enhanced by lust and hostility. He covets wealth through unfair means and passionately pursues the satisfaction of his own desires.   16:12

He says to himself: "This desire is gratified today, another will be satisfied tomorrow; this I have obtained today and another I will fetch tomorrow."   16:13

"This enemy I have killed and the other I will kill; I am the god, the experiencer, the achiever, the mighty, and the enjoyer."   16:14

"I am rich and of noble lineage; I am unique and unlike anyone else; I will perform sacrifices, share my wealth with others, and take delight in all this." Deluded by ignorance, an unsage-like man's mind is preoccupied with these thoughts.   16:15

Entrapped by wrong notions, enmeshed by bewildering images, and driven by lustful cravings, such people fall into lowly hell.[66]   16:16

---

[66]"Hell" is a translation of the Sanskrit word *naraka*. *Naraka* is contrasted with the abode of the supreme self. It also means being trapped into the birth–death cycle.

Overflowing with conceit, stubbornness, vanity, and haughtiness of wealth, they hold celebrations in their own name without following any moral rules.   16:17

Filled with egoism, might, pride, passion, and anger, they hatefully slight my presence in their being and in the being of others.   16:18

I throw these detestable, vicious, and ignoble wrongdoers into the birth–death cycle.   16:19

As they are repeatedly born into the anti-divine state, instead of achieving me, they obtain the lowest state (hell) possible for a human being.   16:20

Lustful passion, anger, and greed are three sure ways to this lowest state. O Arjuna, you must refrain from them.   16:21

A man who abandons these three paths of darkness and works on personal improvement reaches the highest goal.   16:22

He who dismisses the teachings of the holy books and is propelled by his own selfish desires does not reach either perfection or the highest goal.   16:23

O Arjuna, let the tradition guide you in the performance of right action and in the avoidance of wrong action. Therefore, you should perform your worldly duties in accordance with the prescriptive knowledge of the tradition.   16:24

Chapter XVII

Nature of Faith

Summary:

This chapter covers the nature of faith, food, sacrifice, austerity, and gifts. There are three kinds of faith that originate from a man's material nature. They are classified as good (*sattvic*), passionate (*rajasic*), and dull (*tamasic*). Good (*sattvic*) men are devoted to the deities, while the passionate (*rajasic*) worship the spirits and the dull (*tamasic*) pray to ghosts. There are three kinds of food, three varieties of sacrifice, three kinds of austerity, and three types of charity. They are all classified according to the three components of the material reality. Foods that are tasty, bland, and nourishing and are conducive to a long life, mental vigor, and serenity are good. Foods that are bitter, overtly hot or dry and are conducive to sickness and misery are passionate, and foods that are stale, spoiled, and conducive to lethargy and inertia are dull. Sacrifice performed selflessly is good. If it is performed for the sake of a reward, it is passionate. And if a sacrifice goes against the dictates of the holy books, it is considered dull. Austerity performed for its own sake is good; if done for the sake of praise it is passionate, and if intended for hurting oneself or another person it is seen as dull. A charitable act performed without any expectation of favor is good; if it is with an expectation of a future reward, it is passionate; and if it is intended with malice and contempt it is considered dull. This chapter ends with a discussion of the auspicious chant of *Om Tat Sat,* which needs to be uttered whenever the acts of sacrifice, charity, and austerity are performed.

Text:

◆ *Arjuna asked:*

O Krishna, please tell me about those who devotedly worship you but do not follow the instructions of the holy books. What is the nature of their faith? Can it be classified as good or passionate or dull?   17:1

◆ *Krishna replied:*

Now hear from me three kinds of faith that originate from a man's empirical nature. They are good, passionate, and dull. 17:2

The nature of a man determines his faith. A man is defined by his faith. 17:3

Good men are devoted to the gods and goddesses, the passionate worship the spirits and demons, and the dull pray to ghosts and goblins. 17:4

Those who undergo astringent austerities not prescribed by the tradition are propelled by superficiality, egoism, and lust. 17:5

These ignorant ones inflict injury on the various parts of their body and on me, disregarding that I dwell in them. Consider them to have a demonic nature. 17:6

The foods that men like to eat can be classified into three groups. Similarly, there are three types of sacrifice, austerity, and almsgiving. 17:7

Foods that are conducive to long life, mental vigor, strength, sound health, comfort, and happiness are tasty, bland, nourishing, and easy on the stomach. They are loved by the good men. 17:8

Foods that are conducive to discomfort, misery, and sickness are bitter, sour, salty, overtly hot and dry, and are preferred by the passionate men. 17:9

Foods that are left over from a previous night, semicooked, spoiled, putrid, stale, and tasteless are liked by the dull men. 17:10

A sacrifice is good when it is in accordance with the tradition and without any desire for selfish gratification. 17:11

When a sacrifice is performed for the sake of reward or show, it is considered passionate. 17:12

When a sacrifice is done against the dictates of the holy books, without almsgiving, without chanting sacred hymns, and without reverence, it is dull. 17:13

Austerity of the body consists of reverence for the deities, scholars, teachers, and sages; it also involves purity, simplicity, control of sexual desire, and nonviolence. 17:14

Austerity of speech consists of words that do not cause pain, are truthful, comforting, and encouraging, and are trained by the recitation of the scriptural hymns. 17:15

Austerity of mind consists of mental delight, peacefulness, quietude, self-control, and openness of being. 17:16

When these three austerities are undertaken with complete devotion, concentration, and without desire for recognition, they are called good. 17:17

Austerities undertaken for the sake of earning praise, fame, and reverence are called passionate. They are transient and fleeting.   17:18

Austerities undertaken for the sake of hurting oneself or another person are called dull.   17:19

A gift bestowed upon someone who will not return the favor, with the understanding that charity requires giving at the right time, at the right place, and to the right person, is called a good charity.   17:20

A gift given to someone half-heartedly with the expectation of gaining a favor or some reward in the future is a passionate charity.   17:21

A gift bestowed with malice and contempt upon an undeserving person at the inappropriate time and in the wrong place, is called dull.   17:22

The three words of the chant *Om Tat Sat* depict the ultimate reality. They are the original sanctifiers of the scholars, the *Vedas,* and sacrifice. 17:23

The priests begin acts of sacrifice, austerity, and charity by uttering the word *Om.*   17:24

Men who seek salvation without desiring fruit, perform sacrifice, austerity, and charity by uttering the word *Tat.*   17:25

The word *Sat* is used for existence and truth and therefore is employed when an exemplary act is performed.   17:26

The word *Sat* is also employed for firmness in sacrifice, in austerity, and in charity. Any action performed in that spirit is also regarded as *Sat.*   17:27

Whenever sacrifice, austerity, and charity are performed without devotion, they are called *Asat.*[67] They have no worth in this world or in any other world.   17:28

---

[67]*Asat* means "untruth." *Sat* means "truth."

Chapter XVIII

Paths of Renunciation and Relinquishment

Summary:

This chapter deals with many different themes: the distinction between renunciation and relinquishment; nature, types, motivators, fruits, and abandonment of action; three kinds of doers; three types of knowledge, intelligence, concentration, and pleasure; four social classes and their distinguishing characteristics; the nature of obligation and the achievement of perfection through the performance of one's assigned duty; the characteristics of an actionless action; the requirements for achieving the supreme reality; and the nature of a true devotee. All of these issues are discussed in connection with the three components of materiality. The natures of action, knowledge, concentration, pleasure, duty, and the four social classes are completely governed by these three material aspects. Their influence can be transcended by one who is completely devoted to Krishna and performs each action in the spirit of attachment to him. Through Krishna's divine grace, such a person will achieve union with him. After this long discussion, Krishna instructs Arjuna as follows: "If your mind is centered on me, I will help you to overcome all your difficulties. If your ego stops you from listening to me, you are sure to destroy yourself. If you are driven by selfishness and resolve not to fight, your decision will be futile because your nature will impel you to fight. Therefore, bow devotedly to me and take shelter in me. By my grace, you will achieve the eternal and peaceful abode of the supreme self." Arjuna responds: "With your gracious help, my confusion is gone, and firmness is regained. Unencumbered by doubt, I am ready to follow your command." This chapter ends with Sanjaya reporting to the blind King Dhritarashtra that wherever god Krishna and the great archer Arjuna are, there will certainly be prosperity, righteousness, victory, and glory.

Text:

◆ *Arjuna asked:*

O strong-armed Krishna, I wish to learn from you the essential difference between renunciation and relinquishment.   18:1

◆ *Krishna replied:*

The abandonment of an action propelled by desire is called renunciation, whereas the abandonment of the fruits of action is called relinquishment.   18:2

Some scholars emphasize the renunciation of all actions because they regard all actions to be adulterated by desire, whereas others discourage the renunciation of such actions as sacrifice, austerity, and charity. 18:3

Now hear from me the nature of relinquishment, which is made up of three kinds.   18:4

The acts of sacrifice, charity, and austerity should be performed and must not be abandoned, because they cleanse the doer.   18:5

My definitive assertion is that these acts ought to be conducted without any attachment or without any desire for rewards.   18:6

No prescribed duties ought to be abandoned. The giving up of these actions out of ignorance is inspired by dullness.   18:7

Abandonment of actions due to their insurmountabilty or the possibility of physical harm is inspired by passion.   18:8

O Arjuna, any duty performed for its own sake without any attachment or desire for benefits is inspired by good.   18:9

A wise relinquisher, who is devoid of uncertainty and imbued with goodness, is neither repelled by an unpleasant obligation nor attracted to a pleasant one.   18:10

It is impossible for anyone alive to give up action. True relinquishment consists of abandoning the desire for benefits arising from an act. 18:11

The three types of fruits of action, which are either pleasant, unpleasant, or mixed, are accrued by the nonrelinquisher after death, whereas the relinquisher is spared of these.   18:12

O mighty-armed Arjuna, I will teach you the five factors needed for the successful completion of an action as described by the Samkhya philosophy.[68]   18:13

The five factors are the body, the ego, the senses, the motor organs, and fate.   18:14

These five factors propel the body, speech, and mind to perform good or bad actions.   18:15

---

[68]Samkhya is one of the six systems of Indian philosophy. It presents a view that the universe consists of two independent realities of *Purusha* (consciousness) and *Prakriti* (materiality). When *Purusha* and *Prakriti* come together, the entire universe is created. A human being is a combination of these two realities.

Such being the truth, a man who believes that the divine self is the agent of all finite actions is deluded and far from understanding reality. 18:16

He who is free from egoism, and whose intellect is not muddled, kills warriors without slaying them because he is detached from his action. 18:17

The three propellers of action are knowledge, the known, and the knower, and the three ingredients of action are the instrument, the act, and the doer. 18:18

The Samkhya philosophy categorizes knowledge, action, and the agent into three groups. I will describe these to you. 18:19

The knowledge that sees the one reality pervasive in the diversity of existence is called good. 18:20

The knowledge that sees essential differences in diverse forms of existence is called passionate. 18:21

The knowledge that is without any foundation or substance, and fixes itself on one entity by regarding it as all encompassing is called dull. 18:22

An action is good when it is performed with detachment, when it is free from attraction and repulsion, and when it is without any wish for beneficial consequences. 18:23

An action is passionate when it is performed for the sake of beneficial consequences or when it originates from egotistical impulses. 18:24

An action is dull when it is performed thoughtlessly without one's considering its ill-effect, harm, and destructive capabilities. 18:25

A doer is good when he is free from all attachments and egoism, is full of enthusiasm, and is detached from success and failure. 18:26

A doer is passionate when he is entangled in beneficial consequences, is greedy, is violent, and is engrossed in happiness and sorrow. 18:27

A doer is dull when he is mentally unstable, crude, obstinate, ignorant, malicious, sad, and lazy. 18:28

Like other characteristics, intelligence and concentration can be classified into three groups. Let me describe these to you. 18:29

The intelligence that can discern the difference between an act and a nonact, an action that should or should not be performed, an act that ought or ought not be feared, and an action that enslaves or frees one from this world is called good. 18:30

The intelligence that is unable to discern the difference between good action or bad action and between obligatory or nonobligatory work is called passionate. 18:31

An intelligence that is tainted by ignorance and thinks that right is wrong, and good action is bad action, is called dull. 18:32

The concentration with which one disciplines the functions of the mind, the life force, and the sense organs is called good.   18:33

The concentration that aims at securing righteousness, favorable consequences, and happiness for oneself is called passionate.   18:34

The concentration that begets tardiness, fear, worry, despair, and deceit is called dullness.   18:35

Now I will describe to you the three types of bliss that can delight the practitioner and bring about an end to all suffering.   18:36

The pleasure that gushes out of the divine self and first appears to be poison but turns out to be nectar is called good.   18:37

The pleasure that emanates from the contact of sense organs with their objects first appears to be an elixir and then turns out to be poison. This pleasure is called passionate.   18:38

The pleasure that comes from the confusion of the spirit, from sleep, and from tardiness is called dullness.   18:39

There is nothing on earth or in heaven that is not constructed from the three qualities of material nature.   18:40

The scholars, the warriors, the merchants, and the workers[69] are all destined to perform certain duties, according to their natures born out of these qualities.   18:41

The distinguishing marks of a scholar are the ability to control the mind and the sense organs, purity, forgiveness, knowledge, experience, and faith in life after death.   18:42

The characteristics of a warrior are gallantry, boldness, cleverness, determination in battle, generosity, and nobleness.   18:43

The duties of a merchant are agriculture, protection of the cow, and trade. The duty of a worker is to serve the other three.   18:44

O Arjuna, a man achieves perfection by fulfilling his duties. Let me describe to you how this is accomplished.   18:45

[69]Hindus divide their society into four classes: brahmins (scholars), kshatriyas (warriors), vaishyas (traders), and shudras (workers). This fourfold division is justified by the belief that people are born with different abilities due to the predominance of the qualities of goodness, pleasure, and dullness in their personalities. Those who have the excess of good are capable of reflection and thinking, so they constitute the scholarly class. Those with the predominance of pleasure/passion are capable of physical–emotional activity, so they constitute the warrior class. Those with the excess of dullness are incapable of initiating an intellectual or physical action, so they constitute the worker class. And those with a balance of good, passion, and dullness constitute the trader/merchant class. For the efficient running of a society, all the four classes are needed.

By performing his duties, a man worships the all-pervasive creator and thus achieves perfection. 18:46

It is preferable to perform one's own duty imperfectly than to perform someone else's duty perfectly. By performing one's own duty, which is born of one's nature, a man does not earn any future consequences. 18:47

One should not shrink from doing one's duty though it is flawed, since all ventures have their shortcomings like the fire which is marred by smoke. 18:48

In order to achieve the state of actionless action, a man should perform every action with detachment, self-control, and subdued cravings. 18:49

Now I will teach you how you can reach the supreme self, which is the ultimate goal of all human seeking. 18:50

He who has the required qualities for achieving the supreme reality has mental clarity; has controlled his emotions; has cut off the connection between sense organs and their objects; is detached from attraction and repulsion; lives in a solitary place; eats sparingly; has disciplined his speech, body, and mind; is totally absorbed in meditation; is completely detached from the world; and has transcended egoism, use of force, pride, passion, anger, possessiveness, selfishness, and restlessness. 18:51–53

When the supreme self is attained, his being is flooded with serenity. Untouched by grief or lust, equitable toward all creatures, such a person becomes my true devotee. 18:54

Through this kind of devotion, a man who comes to grasp the reality, substance, and truth of my nature is instantly absorbed in me. 18:55

He who performs every action in the spirit of attachment to me achieves, through my grace, the eternal abode of the supreme self. 18:56

O Arjuna, focus your mind on me, and perform all of your actions for my sake. 18:57

If your mind is centered on me, I will help you to overcome all your difficulties. If your ego stops you from listening to me, you are sure to destroy yourself. 18:58

If you are driven by selfishness and resolve not to fight, your decision will be futile because your nature will impel you to fight. 18:59

Though you do not want to fight because of your mental confusion, you will be compelled to do so because of your nature. 18:60

O Arjuna, I reside in the hearts of all creatures and move them by my magical power as if they were mounted on a cosmic wheel. 18:61

Bow devotedly to me and take shelter in me. By my grace, you will achieve the eternal and peaceful abode of the supreme self. 18:62

I have imparted to you wisdom about the most secret doctrine. Now ponder it over and decide for yourself. 18:63

But listen to one more deep secret, which is the highest wisdom. I am giving it to you for your good, because you are my dearest friend.   18:64

By centering your mind on me, devoting your heart to me, sacrificing for me, and offering worship to me, you will certainly be reunited with me. This is my true promise because you are so dear to me.   18:65

If you leave all your obligations behind and come to me with a carefree mind, I will free you from all moral blemishes.   18:66

Do not impart this secret doctrine to anyone who is devoid of austerity, devotion, and attentiveness, or who belittles me.   18:67

He who imparts this secret wisdom to my worshippers and displays supreme reverence for me will certainly be assimilated into my being at the end of his life.   18:68

I regard the service of this man to be superior to that of all others. Such a person is dearer to me than anyone else on this earth.   18:69

I regard the man who learns this discourse between you and me by heart to be offering me the highest devotion through knowledge.   18:70

He who hears this dialogue with complete trust and without ridicule will be salvaged and will reside in the world of the righteous.   18:71

O Arjuna, have you been fully attentive to our discourse? Are you still confused?   18:72

◆ *Arjuna replied:*

With your gracious help, my confusion is gone, and firmness is regained. Unencumbered by doubt, I am ready to follow your command.   18:73

◆ *Sanjaya said to King Dhritarashtra:*

By listening to this glorious dialogue between Krishna and the great-spirited Arjuna, my hair is standing on end.   18:74

By the gracious help of the sage Vyasa, I have been able to hear this secret doctrine of disciplined action from the lips of god Krishna. 18:75

O King, whenever I am able to remember this glorious discourse between Krishna and Arjuna, my heart overflows with bliss.   18:76

And every time I recollect the wondrous cosmic form of Krishna, I am overcome with rapturous delight.   18:77

O King, I firmly believe that wherever god Krishna and the great archer Arjuna are, there will certainly be prosperity, righteousness, victory, and glory.   18:78

Afterword

Interpretations of the Bhagavad Gita

One may ask: Does the *Bhagavad Gita,* which was composed during the fourth century B.C. in India, have any relevance for people of today? The answer is affirmative. The *Bhagavad Gita,* more than any other book, has influenced the lives of millions of generations of people in India. It has been a standard text on Hinduism for centuries. Its influence has been indelibly imprinted on the Hindu character. Since all aspects of the Indian life have been touched by it, some scholars have argued that to understand the essence of the *Bhagavad Gita* is to understand the Hindu mind. For others it is not just a book of the Hindus but of all mankind. It does not present just a religion of a people but the religion of all people. Some critics hold that though it originated in India, the *Bhagavad Gita* is a book that expresses the basic laws of the human spirit. It has appealed to scholars from all areas and to people of all nations. Anyone who has delved into it has found a message that is pertinent to his spirit.

It has attracted the attention of philosophers because of its discussion of the nature of the world and the human being. It has fascinated the religious person for its depictions of the human spirit, the cosmic form of god, and the mystical experience. It has captivated the moralists because it offers a succinct system of ethics. Poets have been struck by its literary style. Minstrels have extolled it repeatedly by singing its verses. The religious practitioners are never tired of offering their devotion to the person of Krishna. And the translators keep on finding new ways of conveying its central message.

It is the most translated book after the Bible. The translations, commentaries, and interpretations have been numerous. In his bibliography on the *Bhagavad Gita,* J. C. Kapoor[70] points out that more than 2000 versions of the text have been published since the first English translation by Charles Wilkins in 1785. The book has been cited 6000 times in more than 50 different lan-

[70]Jagdish Chander Kapoor, *Bhagavad Gita: An International Bibliography of 1785–1970 Imprints* (New York: Garland Publishing, Inc., 1983).

guages. The *Bhagavad Gita* has been translated into every major language. Many important interpreters from the West, which include the transcendentalists, German philosophers and philologists, Christian missionaries, Indologists, Orientialists, Sanskrit scholars, and poets, have been attracted by this book.

What is it about the content and style of the *Bhagavad Gita* that has given it such appeal to a variety of people? Many reasons can be cited for this diversity of appeal.

First, a group of both Eastern and Western scholars believe that the original *Bhagavad Gita,* which was a part of the Hindu oral tradition, was tampered with during its historical development. A number of new verses were added to it due to the influence of Christianity. Therefore, these scholars question the very authenticity of the content of the present-day *Bhagavad Gita,* and this has provoked much study of the *Bhagavad Gita.*

Second, the traditional Indian system of commentary was called the "great sayings" style. It consisted of selecting an important word or phrase from the text and writing a commentary around it. Since the *Bhagavad Gita* contained many "great sayings," this gave rise to a diversity of interpretations.

Third, some scholars believe that the authors of the *Bhagavad Gita,* who attempted to reconcile a number of contradictory ideas, wanted to present a syncretic system of thought in a single text. This syncretic approach may have backfired by opening up the book to a multiplicity of interpretations.

Fourth, the commentators of the *Bhagavad Gita* have been also guided by the literary status of the text itself. The controversy surrounding the *Bhagavad Gita* as to whether it is a mythological or a historical work has been raging throughout its history. Those who have regarded it as a mythological work, have thought of the *Bhagavad Gita* as a story and have utilized the allegorical method to arrive at certain interpretations of the text. But others who have regarded the *Bhagavad Gita* as a historical document have believed that the events described in the book were actual happenings. Their interpretations have been influenced by this historical status of the *Bhagavad Gita.* This controversy has led to multiple approaches to the text.

Last, some scholars believe that the Hindu mind had a multivalent quality that allowed it to tolerate many points of view simultaneously. This special quality might have been responsible for varied interpretations of the text.

In this section, our aim is to offer the views of a number of interpreters. Since our interest lies in reaching undergraduate students and not just scholars, we will offer a few representative interpretations that have had the most extensive influence throughout the history of the text. These interpretations will be presented under four broad headings: classical, modern, contemporary, and recent. The classical section includes the classical Hindu interpretations of Shankara, Ramanuja, and Madhava; the modern section includes the views of Western interpreters such as Weber, Garbe, and Farquhar; the contemporary section gives the views of Tilak, Gandhi, and Radhakrishnan; and the recent section presents the views of Hauer, Eliot, and Bhaktivedanta.

The classical scholars color and enrich the interpretations of the *Bhagavad Gita* by bringing in their own unique understanding of the system of *Vedanta*. The modern Western interpreters see in the *Bhagavad Gita* the influence of Christianity. Contrary to the first two groups, the contemporary and recent interpreters find in the *Bhagavad Gita* six uniquely different messages. Since these twelve interpretations have exerted a great deal of influence on other translators, as well as on a large number of people, the reader will get a fair sampling of the complex nature of the book by reviewing these scholars. We hope, through these interpretations, the student will become acquainted with many unique pathways leading to the text of the *Bhagavad Gita*.

Classical Interpretations

Shankara's Commentary

One of the oldest and major commentaries written on the *Bhagavad Gita* is that of Shankara, composed during the eighth–ninth centuries A.D. Shankara's own philosophical position of Adviata Vedanta influenced his comments on the *Bhagavad Gita*. Shankara believed that Brahman was the ultimate reality, the created world was an illusion, and the inner self (Atman) was identical with the outer self (Brahman).

A person's salvation lay in the realization of the identity between the inner and outer selves. Shankara utilized this position to interpret the *Bhagavad Gita*. Though action was important to control and purify the mind, once that was accomplished and wisdom was gained, action became totally unnecessary for salvation. For Shankara, therefore, the main message of the *Bhagavad Gita* was to realize the unreality of the world of change, of one's ego and all action, and the important role played by wisdom in the attainment of salvation.

Ramanuja's Commentary

Ramanuja, another Vedantist, composed his commentary in the eleventh century A.D. Since Ramanuja developed a different interpretation of the Vedanta philosophy, his comments on the *Bhagavad Gita* are at odds with those of Shankara. Ramanuja challenged Shankara's views on the unreality of the world, the ego, and action. He described the outer self (Brahman) as possessing many attributes. For him, Brahman was not only the creator of the world, the ego, and the soul, but also resided in them. Brahman as the spirit of the world was comparable to the human soul, which was the spirit of the body.

Both Brahman and the human soul were similar in nature because the former resided in the latter.

According to Ramanuja, Brahman was the deity dwelling at the core of each human being. The ultimate goal of human life was to realize this divinity within. Thus, according to Ramanuja's interpretation, the main message of the *Bhagavad Gita* was that this god, which resided at the core of each being, could be realized with the help of total devotion. If a man guided his life by completely devoting himself to the inner divinity, he was assured of salvation.

Madhava's Commentary

Madhava, another Vedantist, wrote two commentaries on the *Bhagavad Gita* during the twelfth and thirteenth centuries A.D. Unlike Shankara and Ramanuja, he presented a dualistic position by regarding god and soul as two different kinds of realities. The identity between the two was impossible. By accepting god as its creator and controller, the soul should constantly seek its source. This experience of the supreme self was available to each man only through complete devotion. Unlike Shankara, who found the path of knowledge as a means to reach the divine, both Ramanuja and Madhva regarded the path of devotion as the true way to salvation and the authentic message of the *Bhagavad Gita*.

Modern Interpretations

Weber's Commentary

Weber was a Christian theologian who was influenced by Lorinser's commentary on the *Bhagavad Gita* written in 1869. Lorinser believed that since the author of the *Bhagavad Gita* had knowledge of the New Testament in the Bible, a number of Christian concepts and ideas were interwoven in the text of the *Bhagavad Gita*. Weber elaborated upon this position by holding that there were apparent similarities between the names Krishna and Christ. Further parallels between the New Testament and the *Bhagavad Gita* could be seen in the stories of the virgin birth, the early lives of Krishna and Christ, and the central place given to devotion in the Bible and in the *Bhagavad Gita*. Since the *Bhagavad Gita* was a part of the Hindu oral tradition, the original ideas of the text were modified to make place for the influence of Christianity.

Therefore, he concluded that the present-day *Bhagavad Gita*, which consists of 700 verses, was of smaller length in its earlier version.

Garbe's Commentary

Garbe, another Christian scholar, believed that at least 170 out of 700 verses of the *Bhagavad Gita* did not belong in the original text. Garbe believed that they were inserted at a later date by the various interpreters. He disagreed with Weber that the concept of devotion was borrowed from the Bible by the author of the *Bhagavad Gita.* Instead, he believed that this notion genuinely belonged to the *Bhagavad Gita.* According to Garbe, the influence of Christianity was evident in other areas. He held the position that the *Bhagavad Gita* had both theistic and pantheistic components. The pantheistic part was a genuine aspect of the *Bhagavad Gita,* whereas the theistic portion was added to the text due to the influence of Christianity.

Farquhar's Commentary

Some Christian theologians were interested in revealing the Biblical influence on the *Bhagavad Gita,* whereas others were more interested in challenging the historical status of the text. The historical versus mythological controversy has divided the interpreters into two opposing camps. Farquhar, who had a theological training in Christianity, gave this controversy a different kind of twist. He tried to show that the life of Krishna was sketched after the historical Jesus of Nazareth. In Farquhar's opinion, Krishna was not a historical figure but a purely imaginary character. He believed that the author of the *Bhagavad Gita* gave to Krishna the same attributes that the historical Jesus possessed. According to Farquhar, the presentation of Krishna as adored by a multitude of devotees, with their unconditional worship directed toward him as a sure means to salvation, indicated characteristics directly borrowed from the life of Jesus. All in all, along with other theologians, Farquhar believed that the original *Bhagavad Gita* was tampered with and a number of new verses were added to the text due to the influence of Christianity.

Contemporary Interpretations

Tilak's Commentary

Bal Gangadhar Tilak lived from 1856 to 1920. His ideas and views influenced the Indian Nationalist Movement in the earlier stages of its development. He wrote the *Gita Rahasya* in 1915, which was an extensive commentary on the *Bhagavad Gita.* In the *Bhagavad Gita* he found the ideas of Indian Nationalism as well as the violent means to overthrow the British government. According to Tilak, though the *Bhagavad Gita* taught three paths of salvation, namely, knowledge, devotion, and action, its real emphasis was on the path of action. The main message of the *Bhagavad Gita* was not to give up action but to perform it with full knowledge and devotion. Action for Tilak was natural to all human beings. Because our ordinary action was guided by desire and ignorance, the *Bhagavad Gita* regarded these two as the real enemies. An action was good when performed under the guidance of knowledge and desirelessness. Devotion and knowledge were the proper ingredients for an action to succeed, but it was the performance of action that took priority over them. Ideal action for the *Bhagavad Gita,* then, was the skillful performance of an action without desire for personal benefit. An action done for the sake of the world's welfare was highly commended by Tilak.

Tilak saw a direct connection between the doctrine of ideal action and the performance of one's caste duties. One must fulfill one's social obligations irrespective of consequences. Tilak drew another conclusion from the *Bhagavad Gita:* He thought that it was the duty of the warrior class to beat the opponent at its own game. According to Tilak, since the British government had used violent and foul means to rule India, it was permitted in the *Bhagavad Gita* to overthrow the British by using similar means.

Gandhi's Commentary

Mahatma Gandhi lived from 1869 to 1948. Like Tilak, Gandhi, who exerted a great deal of influence on the Indian Nationalist Movement, found his inspiration in the *Bhagavad Gita.* Gandhi wrote his commentary in 1929. Unlike Tilak, he found in the *Bhagavad Gita* the message of nonviolence. Gandhi's reading of the text revealed to him the allegorical character of the work. According to him, the major characters of the *Mahabharata* and the *Bhagavad Gita* were not real people. They represented some of the qualities that one should inculcate or reject in oneself.

For Gandhi, the whole battle of Kurukshetra was allegorical in nature. For Gandhi, the *Mahabharata* was a book that revealed the futility of all wars. Gandhi asserted that the reason for any war was a conflict between the forces of good and evil that raged within the psyche of an individual. When not resolved, this conflict spilled over into various kinds of actual wars.

Through his deep study of the *Bhagavad Gita,* Gandhi arrived at some important conclusions. First, the *Bhagavad Gita* was an allegorical rather than a historical work; second, the conflict between the Pandavas and Kauravas was a battle between the forces of good and evil within the body of each person; third, Krishna's insistence upon fighting this moral war referred to the subduing of the psychological conflict within, and not to the fighting of an actual war in the physical world; and last, the total destruction of everybody at the end of the epic *Mahabharata* was the poet's way of showing the futility of all wars. From these Gandhi deduced the conclusion that the main concerns of the *Bhagavad Gita* were inner control, detachment in action, and nonviolence.

When these three were inculcated in one's life, one gained inner peace and determination through which an individual could resist the might of any empire.

Gandhi regarded the *Bhagavad Gita* as his spiritual diary, which taught him the use of nonviolent means to topple the British government in India.

Radhakrishnan's Commentary

Sarvepalli Radhakrishnan, who lived from 1888 to 1975, was trained as a philosopher. He also served as vice president and president of India. As a scholar, he wrote his commentary on the *Bhagavad Gita* in 1947. His book was aimed at countering the criticisms of the Western scholars who believed that the *Bhagavad Gita* lacked a system of ethics.

Radhakrishnan's interpretation revealed that the *Bhagavad Gita* did contain basic principles of ethics, as well as ingredients necessary for a universal religion. However, the greatest contribution of the *Bhagavad Gita* consisted in offering to us the eternal principles of religion and religious life. According to Radhakrishnan, the essential aspects of this universal religion were as follows: First, it focused on the divine spirit; second, it emphasized the importance of a direct experience of the divine; third, it tolerated different approaches; and fourth, it was hospitable toward various paths.

The *Bhagavad Gita* had given us many different paths to reach the divine. Depending upon one's inherent nature, one could follow the path of knowledge or devotion or action to understand and experience this divinity. Thus, according to Radhakrishnan, the religion of the spirit was the greatest contribution of the *Bhagavad Gita*.

Recent Interpretations

Hauer's Commentary

The influence of the *Bhagavad Gita* is also evident in the thoughts and writings of a number of recent authors. We will present the views of three of them. First, we will summarize the position of J. W. Hauer, a German Indologist who wrote a commentary on the *Bhagavad Gita* entitled *An Indo-Aryan Metaphysic of Battle and Action*. It was published in 1934. Though this work made very little impact on people outside Germany, it did influence the thoughts of many followers of Hitler. Hauer regarded the *Bhagavad Gita* as an expression of the Indo-Germanic mentality, which, according to him, was a combination of deep inward reflection and outward action. According to Hauer, an ideal warrior was able to reconcile this tension between the elements of introspection and action. For Hauer, warrior-Arjuna was a genuine representative of the Aryan man. His identity with the other Aryan heroes of the Indo-Europeans epics was obvious because he possessed qualities similar to them, such as his reluctance to fight initially; his willingness to enter into the battle only because of his sense of duty; and his involvement in the war not for personal gain or self-aggrandizement but for the welfare of the majority. Thus, the *Bhagavad Gita* was a treatise on the philosophy of action, which provided the warrior a justification for fighting an ethical war. This kind of interpretation was acceptable because it was in tune with the German mentality of the 1930s. Certain Indian nationalists like Bal Gangadhar Tilak were also in complete agreement with this interpretation. They, too, found a similar philosophy of action in the pages of the *Bhagavad Gita*.

Eliot's Interpretation

T. S. Eliot, one of the greatest poets of the twentieth century, was influenced by the thoughts of the *Bhagavad Gita*. In his famous work *Four Quartets*, the influence of the *Bhagavad Gita* is clearly evident. Eliot's central concern in *Four Quartets* was with the relationship between time and eternity. He raised a number of important questions regarding time, history, eternity, the connection between past, present, and future, the idea of progress, the meaning of life, human history, and the nature of a significant action.

The twentieth-century West had observed revolutionary changes in its perspective on human progress, the meaning of human life, the destructive powers of rationality, and the hollowness of philosophy and Christian theology. Through his poetry, Eliot revealed these changes in the Western worldview. Since the philosophy and religion of the West had displayed their own hollowness in dealing with the absurd existential predicament of the twentieth-century human being, Eliot turned to the Orient and especially to the *Bhagavad Gita* to look for answers. Of the many themes covered in *Four Quartets*, the ideas of cyclical time, life as a journey, death as an ultimate and unavoidable end, time as the preserver and the destroyer, the interconnectedness of the past and the future with the present moment, and the performance of each action with full involvement and yet with self-effacement, were some of the philosophical themes borrowed from the *Bhagavad Gita*.

For Eliot, death was the most certain of human events. Since life was a journey leading toward death, each human being was a voyager driven to this final destination by the push of time. The most effective action then was a selfless action done for its own sake and not for any rewards. This conclusion of Eliot is almost identical with one of the main messages of the *Bhagavad Gita*.

Bhaktivedanta's Commentary

After 1968, it was Bhaktivedanta Prabhupada who was responsible for making the *Bhagavad Gita* popular in the West. He founded the Hare Krishna Movement in 1965. He offered his personal translation of the text, calling it *The Bhagavad Gita As It Is*. He openly criticized other interpretations of the text as being biased because they had no inside knowledge of the tradition. However, he regarded his own interpretation to be an insider's view and, therefore, the most authentic in capturing the essential meaning of the text. Bhaktivedanta believed that the *Bhagavad Gita* was a historical work recording a dialogue between Krishna and Arjuna that actually took place. Since the entire book was the authentic word of god, the text of the *Bhagavad Gita* was not only true, but it was the truth. Bhakivedanta took a hardliner's approach to the *Bhagavad Gita*. His religious position could be summarized as follows: Krishna is the supreme personal god and the ultimate object of our desire; Krishna's nature is bliss-consciousness; this bliss-consciousness is available to every human being; since we are all trapped in the illusory world of matter, we suffer; this suffering can be eliminated through a devotional companionship with Krishna; and this supernal bliss could be realized through dancing and chanting the mahamantra, as well as through participating in the ritualistic prayers of the Hare Krishna Society. This extraordinary joy is assured to devotees who abide by the following ethical rules of conduct: chanting the mahamantra, reading and talking about Krishna, telling the beads, accepting a bona fide spiritual master, fasting on certain days, pledging to sacrifice everything for Krishna, and procreating children for the service of Krishna. This, according to Bhaktivedanta, is the essential message of the *Bhagavad Gita*. Since Charles Wilkins' translation of the *Bhagavad Gita* in 1785, no other translation in the English language has had such an appeal as the *Bhagavad Gita* of Bhaktivedanta. His translation has dominated all others since 1968.

Ethical, Philosophical, and Religious Content

The *Bhagavad Gita* is a multitiered book. It deals with philosophical, religious, social, and ethical themes. The 18 chapters of the book cover these ideas in great detail.

Arjuna's Ethical Dilemma

The *Bhagavad Gita* opens with Arjuna's ethical dilemma, which is resolved at metaphysical and religious levels in the subsequent chapters. Throughout the work, Arjuna is reminded of his caste duties as well as his position in the society. Metaphysical and religious issues offer a structural unity to the entire work. In the first chapter of the *Bhagavad Gita,* Arjuna's chariot is brought between the two armies where he sees his brothers, cousins, relatives, and teachers on both sides. His mind is marred by confusion. He becomes unsure of fighting this war. He asks himself: What will I gain if I perform my caste duty of a warrior, which involves the killing of my evil relatives? What will I lose if I do not perform my caste duty and do not fight this war? His mind undergoes a genuine conflict in which his professional and personal duties clash with each other. At the end of Chapter I, Arjuna is so bewildered and confused that he puts down his mighty bow and refuses to fight. On seeing the disheartened and discouraged Arjuna, Krishna offers a philosophical discourse that gives the former the needed wisdom to resolve his conflict. At the end of the book, Arjuna's confusion is gone and he is ready to fight.

Philosophical–Religious Content

Nature of Human Person

The entire discourse in the *Bhagavad Gita* revolves around a few basic philosophical and religious concepts. Krishna tells Arjuna that a human being is a combination of two selves: empirical and transcendental. Our body, brain, and mind make up the empirical self, whereas the transcendental self is the life force within each person. In contrast to the empirical self, which undergoes birth and decay, the transcendental self is pure consciousness, which is immortal. The goal of life is to understand, develop, and control the empirical self in order to transform it into a perfect vehicle for the expression of the immortal transcendental self.

Empirical Self

Moreover, Krishna tells Arjuna that all human beings are identical because they possess the transcendental self, whereas their differences are due to having an empirical self. The latter is formed from three material–psychological qualities, which consist of good, passion, and inertia. These three ingredients are mixed in different proportions to constitute various empirical selves. Some have the predominance of good, others of passion, and others of inertia.

Four Classes

The classification of the society is based on the predomination of these natural qualities in people. Those in whom good prevails constitute the class of scholars; those in whom passion is predominant make up the class of warriors; those in whom there is an excess of inertia constitute the class of workers; and those who possess a balance of the three qualities make up the class of businessmen. Depending upon the inherent qualities of the empirical self, a person is assigned an appropriate place in the society. By classifying the society in this manner, each person is put in a group where he is best qualified to do the job, as well as to perfect his personality, so as to make it a spontaneous vehicle for the expression of the transcendental self. Thus, both the society and the individual derive benefit from this kind of classification.

Paths to Salvation

According to Krishna, since the goal of life is to experience the transcendental self, it could be accomplished by following the paths of action or knowledge or devotion. These paths are available to people who possess different natural abilities. The path of knowledge is most appropriate for the scholar, the path of action is suitable for the warrior, and the path of devotion is available to both the business man and the worker. If each person follows his respective path with full dedication, salvation is assured.

Path of Knowledge

Krishna discusses the path of knowledge in Chapter II. Finding Arjuna discouraged, disheartened, and confused, Krishna tells him that the wise do not grieve because they know the nature of the supreme self. This self is immortal and resides at the heart of each person. Since death happens only to the body and not to the self, Arjuna's despair is unwarranted. As a creator of the universe, Krishna has assigned to each human being a task that must be fulfilled in his lifetime. Arjuna should understand that Krishna has sent him to kill the Kauravas, who represent evil on this earth. By slaying these warriors, Arjuna will be destroying only their bodies and not their supreme self. Therefore, Arjuna should be guided by this distinction between the body and the self, and ought to become focused in the performance of his duty by fighting this righteous battle.

Path of Action

Furthermore, Krishna tells Arjuna that though this path of knowledge is for the wise, the latter needs it to perform his duty as a warrior. Arjuna's nature is to be a man of action. He cannot reach his salvation without fulfilling his prescribed obligations. However, not every action can lead to salvation. Krishna informs Arjuna that only those actions are liberating that are performed with controlled senses, with detachment, with devotion, and with selflessness. If Arjuna performs his actions as a duty and without any desire for beneficial consequences, then he is sure to achieve his goal of eliminating the evil and of gaining a place in the heavenly abode of Krishna.

Path of Devotion

There is another path available to people who are naturally prone toward the expression of love and care. This is the path of devotion or worship. Any form of devotion to Krishna is amply rewarded. Even the evildoer can be elevated to the status of a sage by offering worship to Krishna with an open heart. Real devotees focus their hearts and minds on him, perform all actions for him, renounce the rewards of their action, hate no one, and show friendship toward all. They spend their lives performing action as a dedication to Krishna. Their minds are constantly preoccupied with him. They sing his praises day and night, are equable in treating friends and foes, demonstrate equipoise in happiness or suffering, and faithfully regard Krishna as their final goal. By setting their heart on Krishna, adoring him, paying homage to him, and making him their highest goal, these devotees will ultimately be absorbed in him. Though all three paths lead to salvation, Krishna tells Arjuna that the path of devotion is the easiest to follow and the surest way to salvation.

Nature of Salvation

What is salvation and how is it connected to the nature of the transcendental self? Throughout the *Bhagavad Gita,* Krishna emphasizes the assimilation of the individual into the supreme self as the goal of human life. The question raised here is: What is this supreme self? The answer is simply that it is the transcendental self within each individual whose real nature is infinite existence, knowledge, and bliss. Once a person realizes or experiences or merges into this transcendental self, he achieves the state of sorrowlessness and is freed from the eternal birth–death cycle.

Four Wants and Four Stages of Life

Though the realization of the transcendental self is within the grasp of each person, a great deal of effort is needed to gain this insight. The *Bhagavad Gita* makes two interconnected suggestions to accomplish this goal. First, it categorizes all human wants or desires under four headings, and second, it divides human life into four major stages. According to the first suggestion, it is believed that all human beings are born to desire pleasure, fame and fortune, righteousness, and complete liberation from all limitations. These four are the basic wants in every person. The first three are related to the empirical self, whereas the last is connected to the transcendental self. The entire development of a human being indicates his lifelong involvement with the satisfaction of these desires. According to the second suggestion, there are four stages of life during which a person can satisfy these wants. Life is looked upon as a gift and an opportunity given to us by Krishna to free ourselves from the clutches of the cycle of birth and death. While we live to satisfy these wants, we also have the capacity to realize total freedom from all limitations. How does one accomplish both of these during one life span? According to the *Bhagavad Gita,* this can be achieved by living the four stages of life according to a prescribed plan. Since life is a gift given to us by gods, our ancestors, parents, teachers, and society, we have obligations toward all of them. By living the four stages of the student, the householder, the hermit, and the ascetic, a man fulfills his duties toward all of them.

During the first 25 years, a man lives the life of a student, and he is a receiver of knowledge. Here he learns from the teacher the knowledge of the scriptures, meditation, and proper conduct. By accumulating knowledge, the student fulfills his obligations toward the teachers and the teaching profession.

At age 25, the student comes back to the society and puts his theoretical knowledge into practice by getting married, by having a family, by taking a job, and by producing wealth for the society. In this stage, the three goals of pleasure, wealth, and fame are accomplished through righteous living. By having children, he fulfills his obligations toward his ancestors and parents. By producing wealth, he performs his duty toward the society.

When a man is 50 years of age and the first grandchild is born, he should be ready to retire from active participation in society by giving everything material to his children. He should move to the outskirts of society by adopting the role of a hermit. Here he ought to try to form a deeper relationship with the rest of the universe by getting deeply involved in the study of the scriptures as well as nature. This can be accomplished through listening, reflecting, and meditating on the world. Here an attempt ought to be made by the individual to cut off his attachments to material things, family, and all possessions. The only contacts that exist with family and other people at this stage should be at a superficial level. When one starts feeling more and more closeness between himself and the universe around, one should cut off all connections with other people by moving into the depths of the woods. Then the individual will feel total oneness with the universe and will be able to realize the union of the inner self with the self of the world. This experience of oneness between oneself and the universe is the final goal of life and is called *moksha*. Once this is achieved, a man experiences the stage of sorrowlessness or total bliss. At death, such a person breaks the cycle of birth and death and is reunited with the creative force of the universe or the supreme self.

If one takes this point of view, the *Bhagavad Gita* becomes a book on social and ethical philosophy that has the goal of offering an individual salvation here and now. Though a great deal of importance is assigned to this kind of participation in the organized society, Krishna tells Arjuna that the final end of life, which is assimilation into the supreme self, can be easily attained by following the path of devotion.

Devotional Mysticism of the Bhagavad Gita

As students, we might be tempted to raise the following question: Is there one central theme in the *Bhagavad Gita* that has been the focal point of discussion among the philosophers and the interpreters? Devotional mysticism comes close to being this kind of theme, and indeed it has been the preoccupation of the major scholars of the text.

The *Bhagavad Gita,* with its dialogical style, simplicity of exposition, and grassroots level of discussion on complex philosophical and religious issues, has been the most popular book of the Hindus. It attempts to reconcile different schools of thought and religious beliefs. In it, the idea of a personal god, Krishna, is introduced. This god is all-encompassing. It is the creator, the preserver, and the destroyer of the universe. All other gods and goddesses are its various manifestations. It is the essence of everything there is. Instead of worshipping many deities or objects, one should concentrate one's energies on one god. Since Krishna is not only the unmanifest but also the imminent god who dwells in everything, he is lovable, personable, approachable, and relatable. The devotee does not have to read difficult scriptures or go through intricate rituals to appropriate him, because he is accessible to anyone who performs an action in the spirit of self-surrender and devotion.

In the *Bhagavad Gita,* devotion is regarded as an unqualified dedication to the person of Krishna. One can relate to him by focusing one's heart and mind on him, by performing an action with the intent of serving him, by renouncing the rewards of one's action, by hating no one, and by showing friendship toward all. Since Arjuna has shown to Krishna that he satisfies the conditions of a true devotee, Krishna reveals to him his cosmic form. This mystical experience assures Arjuna of success in the fulfillment of his earthly duty of fighting the war and of attaining ultimate liberation from the cycle of birth and death.

Glossary

The terms and names listed below have been discussed in the footnotes throughout the text. I have selected the most important or significant terms necessary for an understanding of the text of the *Bhagavad Gita*.

Arjuna: One of the Pandava kings; the great warrior who doubts the reasons for fighting the war.

Artha: One of the four goals of life. It deals with obtaining wealth, name, and fame.

Atman: The inner self or the divine spark that resides at the core of a person's being.

Bhagavad Gita: Literally means "The Song of God." It is also the text of the *Bhagavad Gita,* which constitutes one of the 18 chapters of the epic *Mahabharata.*

Bhakti: Devotion or love. Bhakti yoga is one of the three paths to enlightenment or self-realization.

Brahman: The ultimate reality or the objective universal self in contrast to Atman, which is the subjective self in each human being.

Brahmin: The highest of the four castes in the Hindu system of social classification. Brahmins make up the priestly or scholarly class.

Dharma: Righteousness. One of the four goals of life.

Dhritarashtra: The blind king whose five nephews (Pandavas) and 100 sons (Kauravas) are ready to fight the war of righteousness.

Duryodhana: Chief of the Kaurava princes. His name means "dirty fighter."

Gnana: Knowledge. Gnana yoga is one of the three paths to enlightenment or self-realization.

Gunas: Qualities that are the constitutive elements of all material objects, including the human body and the mind.

Kama: Pleasure. One of the four goals of life.

Karma: Action. Karma yoga is one of the three paths to reach enlightenment or self-realization.

Kauravas: The 100 sons of the blind king Dhritarashtra, who represent the evil forces in the *Bhagavad Gita.*

Krishna: The god-incarnate. Also Arjuna's charioteer, who offers a metaphysical discourse, which constitutes the text of the *Bhagavad Gita.*

Kshatriya: The second highest caste in the Hindu system of social classification. Kshatriyas make up the kingly or warrior class.

Kshetra: The field or vehicle through which consciousness operates in the world. It designates the human body in contrast to consciousness.

Lila: Divine playfulness through which the entire universe is created.

Maya: Cosmic illusion or magic, which conceals the nature of ultimate reality.

Moksha: The highest goal of life. It means freedom from all limitations or salvation from the birth–death cycle.

Naraka: It comes close to the word "hell" and can be contrasted to the abode of the supreme self. It also means being trapped in the birth–death cycle.

Pandava: The five Pandava brothers: Yudhisthira, Bhima, Arjuna, Nakula, and Sahdeva. They represent the good forces in the *Bhagavad Gita.*

Prakriti: The primal material reality or material nature. It consists of the three ingredients of pure joy (*sattva*), restless activity (*rajasa*), and dullness (*tamasa*). Through various combinations of these components, different objects and creatures are formed in the world.

Purusha: The conscious reality that experiences the universe. It is the spark of divinity in each human being.

Purushottama: The supreme person. Since Krishna's real nature transcends both the material and divine selves, he is regarded as the supreme being.

Rajasa: The quality of restless activity or passion. It is one of the three components of the material reality of which all objects, including the human body and the mind, are formed.

Samkhya: One of the six orthodox systems of Indian philosophy. It presents a view of the universe consisting of the two realities of consciousness and materiality. When these two realities come together, the entire universe, including human beings, is created.

Sanjaya: The minister of King Dhristrashtra, who is given the divine sight by the sage Vyasa through which he describes the dialog between Krishna and Arjuna, and the battle to the blind king.

Sattva: The quality of pure joy or good. It is one of the three components of the material reality of which all objects, including the human body and the mind, are formed.

Shudra: The fourth and lowest caste in the Hindu system of social classification. Shudras constitute the workers or the feet of the society.

Tamasa: The quality of pure dullness or inertia. It is one of the three components of material reality of which all objects, including the human body and the mind, are formed.

Vaishiya: The third and the upper caste in the Hindu system of social classification. Vaishiyas constitute the trader or merchant class.

Vedanta: Literally, "the end of the *Vedas*." Contains the essential philosophical ideas of the Vedas.

Vedas: The four earliest books of the Hindus. They constitute the ancient lore that emphasizes rituals to gain access to deities.

Yoga: Literally, "union." It also refers to a system of philosophy that originated in India in 500 B.C., which offered a practical method to reach union between the lower and the higher self.